Praise for *How Do I Get There from Here?*

"The essence of a rich life is knowing that you're fully engaged in a journey that's touched by love, learning, and open to the joy and adventure of the unexpected. George Schofield shows you how to do just that."

—Kerry Hannon, bestselling author of
Great Jobs for Everyone 50+ and *Love Your Job: The New Rules for Career Happiness*

"George Schofield has written a superb life-planning and retirement-planning guide for people over 50. His interviews with insightful experts and fascinating people, talking about the second-act life choices they made, are both fascinating and thought-provoking. Once you finish reading the book, you truly will be able to determine how to become what Schofield calls the 'executive director' of your life after 50."

—Richard Eisenberg, Managing Editor and
Senior Web Editor, Money & Security and
Work & Purpose Channels, *Next Avenue*

"Not so long ago, turning 60 signaled the time was near to stop pocketing a paycheck and to pursue full-time leisure. Yet many Americans are rethinking and reimaging the second half of life by continuing to learn, earn a paycheck, nurture their creativity, and stay engaged with their community. Of course, making transitions is never easy and it's harder than usual for those in the second half of life because many of the old rules don't apply. George Schofield offers a thoughtful and practical guide to help you on your journey. "

hor of *Unretirement*

"At a time when the only predictable thing about 'retirement' is that it involves continuous change, this terrific book offers a fresh and hopeful approach to planning the second-half of life. Based on the author's experience as a developmental psychologist and career expert, it is filled with helpful real-life stories, actionable strategies, and expert insights that are sure to help you thrive during your plus-50 years. "

—Nancy Collamer, author of *Second-Act Careers* and founder, MyLifestyleCareer.com

HOW DO I GET THERE FROM HERE?

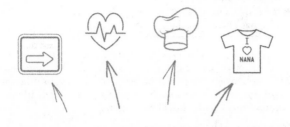

HOW DO I GET THERE FROM HERE?

Planning for Retirement When the
Old Rules No Longer Apply

GEORGE H. SCHOFIELD, PH.D.

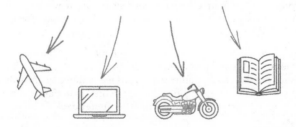

AMACOM

AMERICAN MANAGEMENT ASSOCIATION
New York | Atlanta | Brussels | Chicago | Mexico City | San Francisco
Shanghai | Tokyo | Toronto | Washington, DC

Bulk discounts available. For details visit:
www.amacombooks.org/go/specialsales
Or contact special sales:
Phone: 800-250-5308
E-mail: specialsls@amanet.org
View all the AMACOM titles at: www.amacombooks.org
American Management Association: www.amanet.org

This publication is designed to provide accurate and authoritative information in regard to the subject matter covered. It is sold with the understanding that the publisher is not engaged in rendering legal, accounting, or other professional service. If legal advice or other expert assistance is required, the services of a competent professional person should be sought.

Library of Congress Cataloging-in-Publication Data

Names: Schofield, George H., author.
Title: How do I get there from here? : planning for retirement when the old rules no longer apply / by George H. Schofield, Ph.D.
Description: New York, NY : AMACOM, [2017] | Includes index.
Identifiers: LCCN 2017003347 (print) | LCCN 2017018529 (ebook) | ISBN 9780814438695 (E-book) | ISBN 9780814438688 (pbk.)
Subjects: LCSH: Retirement--Planning. | Older people--Life skills guides.
Classification: LCC HQ1061 (ebook) | LCC HQ1061 .S3434 2017 (print) | DDC
  306.3/8--dc23
LC record available at https://lccn.loc.gov/2017003347

About AMA
American Management Association (www.amanet.org) is a world leader in talent development, advancing the skills of individuals to drive business success. Our mission is to support the goals of individuals and organizations through a complete range of products and services, including classroom and virtual seminars, webcasts, webinars, podcasts, conferences, corporate and government solutions, business books, and research. AMA's approach to improving performance combines experiential learning—learning through doing—with opportunities for ongoing professional growth at every step of one's career journey.

Printing number

10 9 8 7 6 5 4 3 2 1

For my wife: Linda M. de Mello, amazing me every day with her determination and passion for social innovation, high standards, and improving the world we live in.

For my sons and their wives, Todd and Danielle Schofield and Kevin and Jennifer Schofield, who impress me regularly with their abilities and dedication.

For my grandchildren: Laura, Natalie, Holly, Kyle, Sarah, Madison, and Robert Schofield, already determinedly living lives whose present I can admire but whose long-term futures I can only imagine.

ACKNOWLEDGMENTS AND APPRECIATION

If it were not for Debra Englander, my editor, you would not be holding these ideas and this book in your hands or seeing it on your screen. I'm often loquacious. She is often terse. She has extended professional experience I don't have. I have extended professional experience she doesn't have. We found ways to work with, draw on, and respect each other's skills. In all our back-and-forths from concept to book proposal to delivering the completed manuscript to the publisher we never had the tensions that can often surface in such efforts. I'll always be grateful to her for being a total pro. And we've already begun our next book project together. How's that for a testimonial?

The team at AMACOM has been wonderful to work with. My senior editor, Tim Burgard, embraced the concepts in this book and patiently listened to my concerns over the title and jacket design, and along the way, taught me the finer points of the publishing process.

My virtual support team of professionals has been essential to getting this project together and to fruition. Numerous people served in different roles and at various times, some at the beginning, some in the middle, and some toward the end. All made significant contributions. They deserve a special round of applause. My thanks in random order to Linda de Mello, Michelle and Jay Cavallaro, Peter Doris, Rachel Shuster, Siri Allison, Tracy Lamond, Julie Moline, Kim Kildahl, Lanark Lockard, Mary Doan, Ben Gioia, Marshall Moseley, Sally Gallagher, Andrew Salisbury, Daniel Albrecht, Rachelle Pachtman, Rob Nissen, Andy Kefford, Derek Hart, Lou

Heckler, and the staffs of Whole Foods in Atlanta and Ft. Lauderdale whose culinary efforts allowed me to have one decent meal every day of my monastic, consuming, extended writing retreats: a healthy dinner from their hot and cold buffet bars.

I have been fortunate enough at different times and for different reasons throughout my life to receive mentoring from the amazing people I think of as my "Power Women." A special thanks for their enduring impact, in chronological order, to Laura Skinner Polson, Margaret Thaler Singer, Argentine Saunders Craig, Linda M. de Mello, Barbara Hohimer Snider, and Patricia E. "Mi Tei" Bonarek.

I'm someone who can write blogs and articles amidst the daily whirl of life. A book, however, is an entirely different beast. I have had to lock myself away alone to think and write uninterrupted, usually for two to three weeks at a time. Linda Desmarais and Doug Barker made their Atlanta Buckhead condo available to me for the initial writing. My deep thanks to them. Later, Kelly Gorman and Steve Carnevale made their vacation home available to me for the creation of the full original manuscript. My sincere appreciation is extended to them, too.

Also, special acknowledgment and appreciation to:

Andrea Gallagher	Ginny Orenstein
Bevan Gray-Rogel	Green Palm
Bob Seiter	Harry Hobson
Bobbie Berger	Harry Dawson
Carole Lockard	JoAnn Dawson
Charles D. Maurer	Jeff Orenstein
Christopher Mattock	Judith Sedgeman
Daniel J. Martin	Kathy Grant
Dan Schawbel	Kerry Hannon
Dee Albrecht	Kimberly Kollet
Dick Angellotti	Laverne Kusper
Dorian Mintzer	Mary Laxague
Elsie Souza	Michael Alec Rose
Fred Mandell	Nancy Hobson
Gerri Detweiler	Nancy Collamer

Patricia Smith of Le Chateau,
    Buckhead
Rachel Shuster
Richard Bolles
Richard Eisenberg
Rick Albrecht

Rick Deucker
Siri Allison
Sue Seiter
Tony Souza
Willa Bernhard

CONTENTS

HOW DO I GET THERE FROM HERE?

Introduction

The place to begin, as I often say, is where we are. It's fun to imagine the future, and we need to do that, but that imagining frequently fails to become actionable unless we start with and remain candid and well informed about where we really are today. It's too easy to get lost in the joys of possibilities and frequently too painful to look in the mirror and acknowledge where we are. Where are we?

We're generally over age 50 and have some growing level of awareness that we're likely to have a MUCH longer active future in front of us than our grandparents did. If you're age 50 now, that means you could live, have to pay for, and want to find engagement and meaning for another 50 years. Not everyone will live that long, of course, but you should consider this possibility. Those additional 50 years are the equivalent of a lifetime for our ancestors.

Not so long ago, the word "retirement" meant essentially the same thing to everyone. It's as if you said the word "apple." There would be little variation of the apple image across socioeconomic groups and individuals.

Today, on the other hand, if you say the word "retirement," multiple and diverse images spring into mind because while people still aspire to some form of retirement, they're unclear about what is both probable and possible. It's as if you said the word "shoe." There could be endless variations in size, shape, and fit of the shoe image across socioeconomic groups and individuals.

We live in a time in which chronological age is less and less an indicator of who we are. Most of us know old 65-year-olds and young 85-year-olds. What makes the difference in their lives?

We live in an era in which women generate income, participate in building family wealth, and outlive men. They are running households, being caregivers for their own and others' parents, while juggling education, work, and careers. I think they are deserving of special attention and information as we proceed to explore "How Do I Get There From Here?" We also live in an era in which men's lives are much less linear, gender role-driven, and predictable than in the past. This book contains sidebars throughout, some that will resonate more strongly for women and some for men. It's my hope that these sidebars will foster learning for and through each other.

We live in a world in which we still tend to cling to the Four Stage Life Model (1. Childhood, 2. Education, 3. Work and Family, and 4. Retirement) even though there is evidence all around us that for many of us this model is outdated and even dangerous because it leads to expectations and decisions that are no longer realistic.

We struggle with the New Normal vs. the Old Normal. We live in a time of at least as much Disruptive Change as Continuous Change.

We live in a culture that likes short, easy labels and roles that purport to tell the complete story about us at an auditory glance. Dentist. Soccer mom. Plumber. PTA president. Runner. CEO. Straight-A student. Competitive swimmer. World traveler. Voter.

Easy labels are just that: easy. They often aren't particularly true and certainly not complete. There are endless ways we can limit ourselves and our futures by preventing the lights from going on in our heads by allowing others to limit who we are through easy labels and, worse yet, using those same easy labels to establish who we are now and will be in the future.

What would it be like to choose one label only or several labels? How satisfied are you with one label that is presumed by others to tell the story about you? Here's an example of someone whom I truly admire who doesn't easily fit into an easy "label."

Michael Alec Rose has become one of my identity heroes. I experience him as a complex, edgy, warm, funny, earnest, and talented man. He has found ways to combine being a university educator at Vanderbilt with composition of music, fatherhood, professional speaking, and being a spouse with a myriad of other activities and interests. I cringe a bit at using these nouns and adjectives, knowing he will have a sharp rejoinder for me that is both grounded and intellectual.

George: If we wanted to understand who Michael Alec Rose is, where would we start?

Michael: Wow. OK. Well, I guess to work backwards, biographically, because I do think you're right, that we only come to realize things at a certain point long after we are 40, if we're lucky enough to live that long. And we begin to understand ourselves better and more wholly. And I think with more holiness as well!

George: One can hope.

Michael: How to figure out what's sacred, and how to be as generous as possible in defining such a thing. So I am a composer, and I think that what makes my profile as a composer unique, perhaps, at least I hope to think it is unique, is that I don't see myself in the conventional professional way.

Some of that is very willful. I have not made many connections with my fellow composers, who are much more ambitious and much more centrally involved in pursuing careers. I don't have any jealousy about this. Because this is the path that I've chosen for myself just as deliberately as my colleagues have chosen their more obviously ambitious and successful paths. I'm using the word "successful" in a conventional sense.

George: Putting quotation marks around it.

Michael (laughter): Right. So the reason why I think I have set myself apart from the business of being a composer is because I don't see composition—I don't see the act of composing, the daily practice of composing every day—to be something that I can . . . what's the right word? Reify. You know? Actually turn it into a solid thing. It doesn't have any reality for me, apart from the rest of my life. It's a continuum, with all the other things that I love, and all the other things that I do. Of course, most importantly, my job as a husband and as a father. And I know that all composers have to deal with these pressures, and have to find a balance between the work of creating music and of being in the world.

But for me, it feels like the texture of my life is an ongoing refusal to define myself in any way. That's how I define myself. I refuse to be an academic. I refuse to be a professional composer. I refuse to be merely a Jew just because I happen to have been born Jewish. I refuse to be a masculine person, or a male person, because I don't like those gender stereotypes, or constructs. I refuse to be old just because I happen to be 57. It doesn't feel like I'm old. I refuse to be a white person because I'm also a Jew, and have a history with my people having been persecuted apart from the typical white Anglo-Saxon Protestant, or an earlier condition into what you would call the Aryan race.

These rather stubborn refusals to define who I am are somewhat ironically, and without any illusion, a very definite identity that I have constructed for myself.

Plato even talks about it and one of the dialogues—that you have to give 20 years of service first to the community, before you can go and be a contemplative philosopher, or in my case a composer. Now I'm sort of overstating it, and oversimplifying, because of course I was also writing music that whole time. But I think it's only in the past decade or so, after those first 20 years, when I really—with the help and understanding of a wonderful dean at my music school—I was able to make the turn, and truly accept at the age of 45 or 46. And this speaks to your own project here—it was only then that I gave myself the time that I needed to develop fully as a composer.

And the past 10 or 12 years has been an extraordinary adventure of finding my own voice, coming into my own, with the help of dear friends and colleagues—performers who have been the champions of my music. So, I think, to go back to your earlier question: How would I define myself? I'm someone who loves difficulty.

You can learn more about Michael and his music by going to https://michaelalecrose.com/.

We live in a culture with a huge bias for action. Just give me the six steps so I can leap into action. Let me admit here that I have a huge bias for action myself. Frequently my wife wants to discuss a possibility and, out of my bias for action, I often have it done before she has all of the words out of her mouth. This isn't what she wanted at all. She wanted an actual discussion about the possibilities, a definite plan, budget and dates, and the sense of joint ownership regardless of whether she or I did the action. I constantly have to check my bias for action impulse, and listen carefully before leaping into action. Sometimes, I don't catch myself in time but usually I do after all these years together.

Action feels so much better than reflection and worrying about the details. We love to solve problems and achieve goals and move on to what's next. While this may work for fixing a leaky sink, or helping your grandchild get an A on a spelling test, or learning to cook fondue, when it comes to an evolving plan for your life, pursuing it, dealing with surprises, and adapting the plan and ourselves, action is only part of the formula. It's called Your Life for a reason. And it—and you—deserve the best you can provide as you go along.

We live in a culture that focuses on the three steps to do something or the six winning strategies. These immediate word pills can spare us—and deny us the rewards of—the really hard work of figuring it out for ourselves in personalized, smart, and lasting ways.

We live in a time in which long-term planning is increasingly impossible. Instead, we have to become better and better at creating, updating, and adapting not only our plans but also ourselves as we go along.

We live in a highly connected time. Geographic, time zone, local, and national boundaries are highly permeable. In fact, on a practical level, thanks to technologies, the boundaries almost don't exist. Instead of not having enough information, we can actually have too much of it, leaving us both saturated and numbed.

After age 50 many of us have both the broad life experience and the future possibilities ahead of us to be unwilling or unable to fit easily under a single, permanent label like retiree or senior.

In my own case, I'm a developmental psychologist. That usually means the study of children. How does a great five-year-old get to be a wonderful 10-year-old? (Hint: The child doesn't start at nine.) Not in my case. I'm especially interested in developing and growing—skills, expertise, approaches, adaptability—between age 50 and Elderly-and-Needs-Help (as opposed to elderly and still successfully independent), whenever that may be for us individually. How does a great 50-year-old get to be a wonderful 75-year-old? (Hint: You don't start at age 74.) Just because you were good at something at age 30 or 40 doesn't mean it will serve you well at age 55 or 75. The people in your life when you're 45 may not be the people you need around you when you're 70. Who will you need to be to craft a great life? What will you have to be good at? What will you have to leave behind with appreciation because it was valuable but no longer serves you well? Who will you need in your communities and networks? At a time of life when seemingly long-term decisions refuse to stay made or prove to be an inadequate choice, how will you find the necessary ways to adapt yourself and your plan? That's what this book is all about.

If people need clinical therapy—individual, couple, or family—I immediately refer them out to great clinicians. Diagnosis, treatment, and cure (the medical model)—also known as therapy—still have an important place in our tool kits.

If, on the other hand, people are undergoing a transition that is painful but right on schedule (e.g., the kids are leaving and it's painful but supposed to be happening; there is stress because it's beyond time for a large or small career change for your present and your future; we're feeling the exciting and uncomfortable need to begin anticipating life After 50 and what we're going to have to be good at; we're suddenly and sometimes painfully realizing that the people we are hanging out with now are not, and should not be, the people we will need to be with at age 70; we need to finally begin to stimulate our dormant creativity and ambitions), these are developmental opportunities. Challenging who you are, acquiring new skills and viewpoints, letting go of some of the old ones, and developing a number of alternatives for yourself, leaving behind what will no longer serve you well while creating space for new things to come in your life, these are what can make After 50 great. Therapy may not be the answer if the life transition is right on schedule with or without your permission.

Just because we were good at something earlier in our lives doesn't mean it will serve us well after age 50. In fact, it might get in our way. I'm most interested in those developmental situations, those life transitions that have little if anything to do with the medical model—diagnosis, treatment, and cure. Instead I'm devoted to the ongoing and evolving acquisition and development of skills, strategies, networks, and meaning that will best serve us as we age.

This reflects, of course, the reality that the old model of retiring and then coasting slowly downhill through golden years of leisure until death takes us is essentially over for many of us. Not only are we going to live longer, need more money to do so, and require continuing engagement and meaning in our lives, but this is happening at a time when, for many, permanent and full retirement won't be an appealing or viable option. It's entirely possible that in the future we will have two classes of people:

1. Those who retire entirely and have more than enough money to afford to do only what they want to do indefinitely, without paid work being a part of it. There will be such people and circumstances but they might very well be in the minority.
2. Everyone else. The most successful in this group will begin early, plan incrementally, adapt regularly, and create over time their own unique "right retirement fit."

I'm also an organizational psychologist and a working entrepreneur. I'm a formerly divorced man who raised his sons alone at a time when the societal norm was that a man couldn't raise children well and a woman couldn't be an effective CEO. I was divorced for a long time and have been remarried for a long time, as well. I'm also a speaker/author. I also have some rental properties and manage the managers. I'm a grandfather of seven. I do vocational expert witness work. I'm in the midst of designing a digital game with a friend. I'm writing another book with more planned down the road. I ride my new bicycle, by far the most expensive one I've ever had, farther than I could have 15 years ago. I'm a husband and a partner. I'm a volunteer board member. I'm a Sogetsu Ikebana Sensei. Which label box should I choose? None. My time for single boxes and primary labels is done. My lifeline, as you can see, hasn't been continuous or without curves. I suspect your lifeline wasn't all that straight either. Chances are there is more to you After 50 than a single label can contain. Plus, given 50 or more years of life experience, you aren't easily going to meet someone else's need to categorize you for easy reference with a single label.

We in this After 50 demographic have a huge opportunity and responsibility. Many of us are realizing that, however linear or nonlinear our lifelines were in the past, our futures will be full of surprises. Many of us are going to live a very long time, perhaps 50 years or more beyond age 50.

Whether we live two or 50 years longer than expected, we face a crucial question: Do we want to add those additional years to the middle of our lives or to the end of them? The importance of our personal answer to this question and the decisions we make as a result cannot be underestimated.

We're going to need the money to pay for the additional years, a plan for our lives that can and will adapt as we go along, and a new paradigm that's more about life satisfaction and less about endless goal achievement and bias for action. Doing this will require developing new skills, approaches, and adaptabilities.

What can we do to take responsibility now? What do we need to understand now that will be of maximum benefit and utility for us in the future? Who will be our companions who will help us learn and adapt even as we do the same for them? A reminder: This book is primarily for people between age 50 and elderly. What do I mean by that?

Fifty is clear and arbitrary. It's about the time many of us come to the end of some of our roles—custodial parent, youthful athlete, devoted employee—and begin to not only question the right fit for us but begin to pursue other options. Fifty could be around age 50, 45, or 55. You'll know who you are when you want to leave some roles or some of them leave you with or without notice or your permission.

Elderly is, in my opinion, not definable by chronological age. In fact, when you think about it, aging isn't really the point. Quality of life is the point. Lots of companies sell us products and services, all framed by what a problem aging is for us regardless of whether this is true for us individually or not. I don't even like the word *elderly* but am using it in the absence of a better one. I'm not so crazy about the word *senior*, either. In fact, I think our language has failed to keep up with the pace and realities of individual and demographic change as we, our country, and the world ages.

Is someone elderly because he is age 90? Is someone elderly because she is age 70? We all probably know 70-year-olds who act in some way that we consider elderly. We also all probably know 90-year-olds who do not act in a way we think of as elderly. Elderly, for me, will be that point at which I will have to say to my wife or to my sons, "I need help here. I can no longer be fully self-managing." Or they will have to say it to me. I hope that we are all able to acknowledge that, whenever it is, it will be natural and right on schedule—not fully within my control but not without my influence, either.

A SPECIAL NOTE ABOUT "TRANSITIONS"

 Many of us are accustomed to thinking and talking in terms of "transitions." For want of a newer, more accurate term I'll use the word as part of the conversation you and I will be having in this book. In quieter times of predominantly Continuous Change, transitions often occurred individually. We could clearly see the beginning, the middle, and the end. Example: Joe and Amy had been a married couple for five years. Then they decided to start a family, a significant transition. The beginning of the transition: getting pregnant. The middle of the transition: pregnancy. The end of the transition: bringing their newborn son home from the hospital. Joe and Amy would experience many transitions, a bit spaced from each other, throughout the growing-up years of their son and, later, both of his sisters. Each of the transitions had a clear beginning, middle, and end. Joe and Amy were able to see the transitions more clearly because each was distinguishable from the others.

Discontinuous Change isn't brand new. It has always been with us but not in such profusion or spaced so closely together and overlapping. The presidential race of 2016 and its aftermath may serve as a powerful example. With the increase in Discontinuous Change in our lives and our environment, "transitions," in my opinion, has become a less useful concept. In fact, it has become a somewhat quaint and dated construct. Why? The pace of change has increased. Multiple, demanding transitions can occur, overlapping and tightly spaced. If several transitions are occurring at once, are interrelated, and can't be broken down into clear beginnings, middles, and ends (or it isn't useful to try to pull them apart to see the three segments), we will have a more difficult time analyzing what is really happening and what to do about it.

Joe and Amy's son left for his freshman year of college across the country. He had always been around to open tightly lidded jars and carry the heavier grocery bags for his mother. Also, he served as a kind of surrogate father to his younger sisters during Joe's frequent and extended business trips. Later in the same week, Joe received the surprise news that his division was being eliminated and Joe would lose his job. Three days later, Amy, distracted, accidentally started a fire in the kitchen that almost burned down the house. The older of the two daughters, complete with shiny new driver's license, was rear ended (not her fault) and experienced shoulder and neck injuries. The next day, the for-profit university where Amy had been taking classes—in anticipation of needing additional income for the kids' college expenses—filed for bankruptcy and announced it was shutting down.

Of all of these overlapping and densely packed changes and transitions, only their son going off to college could be seen clearly in advance and was a form of Continuous Change. The others were all forms of Discontinuous Change and transitions. Pulling them apart and finding ways to cope with each of them through identifying beginning, middle, and end was simply not going to be as useful as it was in previous, slower times. What's my point? I recommend that we 1) understand and use "transitions" thinking wherever it will be useful but 2) realize that it may have its reasonable limits in our increasingly change-oriented world and that we have yet to develop a new model for deconstructing multiple, overlapping Discontinuous Change as a way of coping and problem solving.

I've written this book for you and for myself. We're "transitioning" from our traditional and previous roles and age-driven norms without exactly knowing where we're going or what the world is going to be like. We're going to encounter moving targets and winding roads. We need plans. We need to NOT feel like failures if parts or even most of the plan don't work out, whether changes were forced upon us or we changed our minds. We need to know that success lies in our ability to adapt the plan and ourselves to match evolving reality, probability, and our anticipated preferences.

The best choices available to you down the road may not be the same as the ones available now. The best choices available to you may not include a solitary option such as a specific job or one location and might not be answerable with a yes or no answer. The finest choices for you may have a limited shelf life and not be permanent. The most workable choices for you may be several selections you piece together as if you are traveling down the road with some straightaways and lots of curves, too, often unexpected.

There will be a menu of choices. We can greatly influence what's on the menu if we're paying attention and doing the planning, living, and adapting. If one big choice is the best for you AND is available, that is great. If not, don't think you have failed. Begin to gather the best pieces together into a shape that works well for you in the short run and can be modified as you go along.

The best choices you see now may be fleeting. In fact, as we get older, there is an increasing probability that choices we make will be made as part of a series rather than as independent/

free-standing, permanent decisions. We won't have the satisfaction of saying to ourselves, "Whew. That's decided forever. I won't ever have to worry about that one again."

Our heroes are often no longer the people who "made it" early and retired to live a life of fun and leisure indefinitely. Instead, our heroes seem to be those older people doing amazing things with their lives whether they have "retired" forever from paid work or not . . . and often not.

The goal is a high-quality and satisfying life, one fraught with humanity and surprises and learning you can be proud of and enjoy on a daily basis until the end.

If your image of a satisfying life is dominated by extended leisure time and few commitments to yourself or others, perhaps with significantly diminished ambition and curiosity, this book probably isn't for you.

I'm an ambitious guy, myself, eager to lead a really satisfying life each day. I want to do some things I didn't have the time, energy, or life space to do earlier in my life, like writing this book, forming memories with my grandchildren, and creating income streams that are long term so that we're not simply living on savings and Social Security. I'm ambitious to be more creative than I've ever been. I'm ambitious to face every type of change head-on and adapt both my plan and myself accordingly with grace. I'm not checking things off a bucket list; my ambitions are woven into the demands, activities, and leisure of each day—my idea of a highly satisfying life regardless of age.

My own core strategy is having multiple, overlapping professional and personal interests and commitments that require my attention and that produce energy, which can then be used toward each of the others, a kind of symbiosis of interests and activities. No single one is allowed to take up so much of my life space—except temporarily such as writing and completing this book—that it suddenly owns me instead of the other way around.

I don't want my future to be locked in by and limited to the structures, consequences, and outcomes of my past. I want to be clear about what I'm bringing with me from my past—the most useful for my future and what I love the most that can realistically be a part of my future. I also want to honor—and release with appreciation—everything else. I can't bring it all. It's too heavy and bulky. And in many cases it's too dated and comfortable.

I expect to leave the nest, my comfort zone, regularly for an hour or a day or a week, sometimes voluntarily and sometimes involuntarily. I also plan to come back to the nest but not as precisely the same person without any new experiences and insights. And the nest may not be exactly the same, either.

If all of this interests you, you're in the right place. And the information in this book is for you.

At various points in the book I will ask you to stop and complete an exercise. I recommend you do these exercises when you first read them to maximize your learning and enjoyment of the rest of the book.

chapter 1

What You See Ahead of You Depends on What You're Looking for and How Far Away You Are

Choose something to admire. It could be a flower, a football game, a friend, a plate of French toast, or anything else on which you would like to focus for the moment. Made your choice? Great!

Now, in your mind's eye, put it as close to your nose as possible. What do you see?

Again imagine the same thing but place it as far from your nose as possible while still retaining the ability to see the object and distinguish its major parts. What do you see?

Finally, in your mind's eye, move it to that spot in the middle ground where it's clearest to you at that distance. What do you see?

You have just experienced perspective. Did you stand close enough? Did you stand too far away? Did you pay attention to the middle distance in your field of vision? Where you are standing in relationship to what you are looking at can make a huge difference. Of the three perspectives you tried, which was the most informative in this case?

There isn't one right perspective. In life, in order to really see and understand what we're looking at, we're often called upon to see and hold multiple perspectives simultaneously.

Try the same three perspectives with your own aging. What do you see and what do you infer or understand from that?

Now try the same three perspectives with your potential retirement. What do you see and what do you infer or understand from that?

Now try the same three perspectives through the lens of your life planning. What do you see and what do you infer or understand from that?

Henry David Thoreau is quoted as saying, "The question is not what you look at but what you see." I would argue that the question is not only what you see but also what you infer or understand from what you saw. That inference and insight is essential to effective adulthood because it can drive both belief and behavior consciously and unconsciously for a long time.

Let's set aging and retirement aside and use those three perspectives to examine ourselves as an After 50 demographic.

A LOOK AT OURSELVES FROM A SIGNIFICANT DISTANCE

According to the U.S. Census Bureau and AARP, we are a population of 108.7 million people age 50 plus, of which 53.5 million of us are women and 55.2 million of us are men.[1]

The "Baby Boomer" group of people born between 1946 and 1964 totals 76.4 million. There are 32.3 million "Traditionalists" born before 1946.[2]

Our 50-plus population will continue to grow by 19 million people in comparison to an expected 6 million increase for the 18–49 population. This has significant implications for our so-called entitlement programs such as Social Security.[3]

Our average 50-plus household population is 2.35 people, suggesting the kids have mostly moved on, at least for now.[4]

Seventy-five percent of us are white/non-Hispanic, 10 percent are African American, and 9 percent are Hispanic. Shortly, the 50-plus Hispanic population will equal the African American population at 12 million.[5]

According to the 2016 Employee Benefit Research Council Retirement Confidence Survey, 27 percent of us are working in retirement.[6]

A December 2014 Society for Human Resource Management (SHRM) study explored the reasons employees age 55 plus retired from one employer and then went to work for another one. Their reasons for working were: money (72 percent), enjoyment/occupying time (58 percent), health-care benefits (45 percent), and social interaction (42 percent).[7]

In a 2014 Merrill Lynch Work In Retirement study, in partnership with Age Wave, 52 percent of working retirees said they took a break of an average of 29 months after retirement to relax and recharge before going back to work for an average of nine years.[8]

According to research from JP Morgan, men age 65 today have a 78 percent chance of living another 10 years. Women age 65 have an 85 percent chance.[9]

A 2014 survey by the Employee Benefit Research Institute suggests that only 44 percent of U.S. households have tried to calculate how much they will need to save for retirement. The Employee Benefits Security Administration predicts that you will need to have 70 percent of your pre-retirement income available each year after retirement to maintain your standard of living when you stop working. If your pre-retirement income was $80,000, this would mean you would need $56,000 per year from all sources of funds for the rest of your life. If your pre-retirement income was in the lower spectrum, you will need 90 percent. This means that if your income was $27,000 before retirement you will need $24,300 per year from all sources for the rest of your life.[10]

The U.S. Government Accountability Office (GAO) 2015 study shows that about half of the households with people age 55 and older have no retirement savings. Retirement savings are an indicator of other financial resources as well, whereas absence of retirement savings suggests few if any other financial resources. Social Security provides most of the income for about half of households with people age 65 and older.[11]

Reader Exercise

Stop for a Few Minutes to Look More Closely At:

1. Where you fit into the statistics above.
2. Where you don't fit in at all.
3. What's a surprise to you about what you've seen?
4. Where you would like to fit in the future.

. . . .

A LOOK AT OURSELVES FROM A MID-RANGE VIEW

Generation-based labels and constructs are clearly popular and in common usage: Silent Generation/Traditionalists (born 1900–1945), Baby Boomers (born 1946–1964), Generation X (born 1965–1980), Millennials (born 1981–2000), and Generation Z (no consensus on beginning or ending birth year).

There are approximately 55 million Traditionalists living in the U.S. today, allowing for deaths and immigration.

Frequently used characterizations of the Silent Generation/ Traditionalists are respecting authority, duty bound and rule oriented, dedicated to giving back, loyalty, emphasizing law and order, desire for power/status/achievement, and believing in personal responsibility.

There are approximately 76 million Baby Boomers living in the U.S. today, allowing for deaths and immigration. They represent close to one-quarter of the estimated 2012 U.S. population of 314 million people.[12]

Frequently used characterizations of Baby Boomers include transformational, optimistic, question everything, team oriented, wanting to make a difference, personal growth/gratification, challenging authority, competent, ambitious, and believing in "act now, the money will follow."

I am emphasizing all of this because, in addition to other reasons, we represent a huge financial and business opportunity for an unending combination of companies that want to sell us goods or services and scammers who simply want to rip us off. What is the primary way they work on us? It's not dissimilar for the legitimate sellers and the real scammers: They use the art of entertainment and distraction through provocation. The legitimate sellers entice us by selling us the sizzle. Do you really need to buy a ring or a tool you've seen on television for the fourth time this month? Is it really worth it to you to get free name imprinting on your golf balls when you buy a huge quantity? The legitimate sellers share a provocation technique with the scammers: fear. How can you possibly live with yourself and hold your head up to others when you are suffering from erectile dysfunction, dry skin, ring around the collar, falling, or any provoking ad that begins with "Don't let this happen to you!"

Why am I carrying on about this here? Because this book is all about helping you successfully move into the new world of planning and living when so many of the rules no longer apply and won't ever again. How we handle purchase and decision situations involving sellers/scammers can be a predictor of how well we will handle all of the decisions, situations, and opportunities that are going to happen in our futures, including retirement.

Raise your hand if you believe that your birth year is the primary determiner of who you are.

Raise your hand if you believe that there is a low level of diversity among people born between 1900 and 1945 so that they can be easily and readily captured as a homogenous group.

Raise your hand if you believe that there is a low level of diversity among people born between 1946 and 1964 so that they can be easily and readily captured as a homogenous group.

Why is this important? Because subscribing to groupthink about birth-year labels can automatically limit your options and creativity as you move into your own aging and retirement. Who we are and who we have become depends on three features:

1. Birth year
2. Where we were raised
3. How we were parented

Arsenio, born in 1966, grew up in a large, raucous New Orleans family. There were always older cousins plus aunts and uncles to keep tabs on him and his siblings. In many ways his maternal grandmother, always nearby, was the dominant adult of his childhood. His parents, both hard workers but not college educated, were determined that he would not only get a college degree but that he would earn it from a big-name school. As a consequence, his schoolwork and progress were monitored much more closely than that of most of his friends. Sometimes he thought it was a burden, but mostly he experienced it as reliable love for him. He did go to a good college and has built a fine professional career since then. Arsenio does regret living so far from his family now.

Michelle, born in 1966, grew up in Albuquerque. Being fully bilingual, her language abilities were often sought out for translation and letter composition by Spanish speakers in her neighborhood. Her parents, especially her father, were fiercely committed to her developing a combination of self-esteem, diverse interests, good education, and the ability to move gracefully across the many social community boundaries in her native city. Eventually she became an activist and executive director of a local nonprofit. Sometimes it's a struggle to balance her work time with her husband and kids, but she loves her life most days.

Randi, born in 1966, was raised in Manhattan. She went to camp as a girl at a lake in the Adirondacks and her parents took her every other year to Florida to see her grandparents. Her mother, a great lady, was a museum volunteer and a strict Catholic who raised her daughter the same way. Her father was an agnostic who worked most of the time. Their shared loves as a family were theater and classical music performances. Until she went away to college in Ohio, New York and Florida were her geographic world. In college she met and fell in love with a fellow student from Brussels. Eventually they married and now live in his home city.

Rob, born in 1966, was raised on the family farm in Kansas. He loved sports and was very active in Future Farmers of America. His parents were both active church members, and Bobby and his two sisters grew up with a strong sense of family loyalty, cohesiveness, and right and wrong. Until Bobby won an FFA-related trip to California at age 15, he had never been out of the Midwest. To his parents' and his girlfriend's alarm, he fell in love with California and declared his interest in going to one of that state's universities. When he was 19, going to school in California on a sports scholarship, he realized he was gay. It changed his life.

Were Arsenio, Michelle, Randi, and Rob all affected by the major events in both this country and overseas that they lived through between 1966 and today? Of course they were, and they undoubtedly share preferences about life as a result. Is their birth year enough to cluster them together as a uniform quartet? I doubt it.

Reader Exercise:

Stop for a Few Minutes to Look More Closely At:

1. What were the most lasting effects of where you grew up on your worldview and what you consider possible for yourself?
2. What have been the most lasting effects of the U.S. and world history you have lived through?
3. In what ways do you still reflect and practice how you were raised?
4. What facets of you come from deep inside you and have always been strong enough to persevere in the face of resistance and obstacles?

A LOOK AT OURSELVES FROM UP CLOSE

Each of us uses life models, sets of structures, and expectations that make things make sense to us. They are very personal and dear to our hearts. One of the most common is the Four Stage Life Model. It's linear, predictable, we're used to it, and anything else seems either unnatural or weirdly unacceptable. Most of us are so accustomed and attached to our models that we don't see them anymore. They can act as our life's foundation and we use them to set our expectations and behavior. It's like driving to or from work and, upon arrival, not remembering seeing any of the streets or traffic lights; we're on autopilot. At the autopilot stage our models can turn on us quickly without our even being aware of it.

The Four Stage Life Model looks like this:

1. Childhood
2. Education
3. Work and Family
4. Retirement

It seemed to work so well for our parents and grandparents. But our world is very different from theirs. So is this model obsolete?

For many, if not most of us, I believe the answer is a resounding yes.

Why? Let me count some of the ways:

1. Many of us are living far longer than our parents' generation, and with those additional years (even decades) our needs and expectations will be different than in generations past. Will you live longer and healthier than your parents?
2. Living longer will require engagement and stimulation for more years than previously assumed.
3. Living longer will require more money over a longer period of time to support us, keep us active, keep us housed and fed, and keep us healthy.
4. The famous financial planning three-legged stool may require a fourth and a fifth leg. The first leg, the planned benefit retirement with pensions, is growing scarce and potentially unreliable over a course of many years. The second, Social Security, could be at risk, at least in the form it is now. The third leg, retirement savings, is, in the majority of households, grossly insufficient. The fourth leg is one or more additional, if small,

active and passive income streams that are begun long before retirement. The fifth leg is adequate insurance coverage for health and for our survivors who may not be able to jump quickly into the workforce if necessary. Do/will you have all of the legs in place and absolutely assured? How long will you have to work at what you are doing now? What kind of additional income streams can you create now so they can be built upon before or after retirement?

5. The elimination of entire segments of jobs, companies, and industries puts income security at risk. It also puts professional identity, work-related belonging, and the opportunity to be employed again at risk. What we studied in college and learned in the jobs we later held are no longer a guarantee of employability in the future. How solid is the match between your skills/expertise and the emerging, in-demand jobs/gigs in today's world of work for pay? What have you done to update your employability and skill set if you want or need to return to some form of work eventually?

6. Many of our institutions—marriage, churches, health-care systems, employee/employer partnerships, governments—have transformed, and in so doing weakened traditional safety nets. With later-in-life divorces on the rise, the perceived value of churchgoing on the wane, health-care costs rising, employers showing little loyalty to employees, and government programs inadequate, that support has weakened. Institutions have their membership, financial, and commitment limits. Can anyone or any institution be more responsible for you than you are? Upon which institutions can you depend for your future?

If the Four Stage Life Model is outmoded, what should take its place?

I propose a six-stage model:

1. Childhood
2. Work/Education
3. Work/Family
4. Work/Extended Midlife

5. Work/Leisure, and
6. Needs Help Elderly

What? No retirement? How unfair! Well, not really. Let's get real here, one stage at a time.

CHILDHOOD

Childhood used to be simple to identify. Children were young and shorter and less mature. And with years and height and experience, they grew out of it. And, they left home. Now it's much more complicated. Kids move out and often move back in, but not always alone. Employment problems, financial difficulty, marital problems, and saving money for education are only a few contributing factors. While these kids may also be grown-ups, and living with parents on an extended basis prolongs the parent/kid bond, the jury is still out on the long-term impact on both the adult children and the aging parents. For our purposes I would like to define children as those dependent upon their parents for financial support, food, shelter, and guidance about crucial life choices, regardless of age. Still, I think childhood is a valid life stage even if it is dramatically extended through significant, elongated dependence.

WORK/EDUCATION

Take a hard look at the price, value, and impact of a college education, which is more expensive than ever. Many people think student debt and the greatly reduced ability to support oneself when paying off student loans is the single largest obstacle to moving on into more advanced maturity. Education now includes a shorter shelf life of knowledge acquired upon graduation because of the pace of change. Many students are working AND going to college. This prolongs greatly what used to be the launch at graduation: off on his or her own at last.

WORK/FAMILY

Clearly the family norm, by any current and valid statistical measure, is no longer Dad, Mom, 2.5 children, a dog, and a cat. Families have multiple, simultaneous work and careers. Divorce exists all around us as do single-parent households. Kids have activities that may or may not mix part-time work with ongoing schooling. Work doesn't only look like a job anymore. It can also look like freelancing, project work, entrepreneurial efforts, and multiple gigs instead of one employer with one job. Almost no one, except possibly those owning their own small, stationary businesses, will work for one company or stay in the same job for years. Going back to school to update our skills periodically across our lives is going to be increasingly common. Without it we will slip from employable to unemployable, often without noticing it.

WORK/EXTENDED MIDLIFE

If we're going to live longer and healthier, we have a choice to make. Do we want to add those years to our elderly period or would we like to add them to our midlife? I vote for midlife because I firmly believe that the period between age 50 and elderly can be the most rewarding of our lives. We can do some of the most significant, creative, meaningful things in our lives at this time. We may not be slowing down as we age, but there will be a shift in the balance between work (freelancing, entrepreneurial efforts, and jobs) and leisure (volunteering, individual creative projects, athletics, hobbies, travel). There will certainly not be a dead stop, as in one day fully employed, next day fully retired. We'll still be driven by the need for an income stream, extended belonging (which we often find at our place of work), meaningful engagement, and ongoing intellectual stimulation.

WORK/LEISURE

We have an opportunity later in our lives to create a smoother and easier flow between work and leisure. Hopefully we are more comfortable in our own skins, seeing work and leisure less as competing opposites and more as permeable containers with energy, attention, and satisfaction flowing back and forth between them like one of Rudolf Steiner's Flow Forms.

NEEDS HELP/ELDERLY

We may not be the first to realize we've reached the point where we need help in one or more aspects of our lives. Or we may. Regardless, denial may arise. We may not want to recognize it and neither may our loved ones. Reality may intrude. I think it's a skill, certainly a graceful skill, to listen well to someone who thinks we need help—or to ask for it when we realize we need it—and then make a clean, informed decision about it. The distribution of our lives over a potentially longer time frame will require reorienting ourselves to altered realities and needs. It will also mean surrendering models that are obsolete, and that can take tenacity and courage.

Reader Exercise:

Stop for a Few Minutes to Really See Our Primary Models and Their Efficacy

1. What is the primary life model you are now using? No model is, of course, a model in and of itself.
2. What changes are happening in your life that you didn't anticipate?
3. What adapting are you now doing to keep your life plan current and on target?

It's my expectation that getting into the habit of having and using more than one perspective regularly is going to be a life skill that, although it's work to do, is much more likely to result in a high quality of life. I invite you to revisit this chapter whenever you catch yourself relying on a single perspective and suspecting, even half-heartedly, that more than one perspective might give you the information and answers you need.

My sincere thanks for your interest, engagement, and tenacity. These traits should serve you well as we go forward.

And now . . . onto Today's New 50-plus Lives.

Chapter 2

Today's New 50-plus Lives

L ife is full of transitions. As a child you start going to school, moving up from grade to grade, until you enter college and then perhaps move onto graduate school. Afterward, you get a job that lasts for many years and then you land other positions at the same company or possibly a new one, climbing the reliable ladder. You start a family and you settle into a routine. You buy a house. Eventually your kids grow up and have children of their own. Sometime after that you retire with a pension at age 65, have 10 to 15 golden years of leisure, and then die.

Although this description of life may seem familiar and comfortable, it is no longer accurate, if it ever was the total norm. It belongs in the category of myths including: "Christmas Is the Happiest Day of the Year," "Family Reunions Are Always Fun," or "I'm Always Loyal to My Huge Employer and It Is Always Loyal to Me."

Three of the things that are REALLY different about our After 50 futures today:

1. We may live a little or a whole lot longer than we expected or planned.

2. Our futures may not—either by choice or what is forced on or required of us—be an older, extended version of our earlier lives or our parents' experience.
3. Living and being active much longer will require more money, conscious engagement, development of interests, extended good health, and adaptability.

GEORGE'S STORY

I tell this story as an example. I may be an expert, but like everyone reading this book, I am also a person 50 plus, a searcher for great fits for my life, an incremental planner, and an adapter. No one, including me, lives a life that goes in a straight line from birth to death. Take a look at your own life. It will have periods of straightaways interspersed with curves and periods that seem made up entirely of curves. You will have chosen some of these curves. Some will have appeared unannounced and without your permission.

I grew up in a post-WWII culture of rules centered around table manners, good grades, being popular, NOT being different, being polite, avoiding discussing controversial or uncomfortable subjects, and adhering to very strict age-related roles. My parents had clear expectations of what a good boy looked like, sounded like, and how he behaved at all times. You grew up and somewhere in your 30s you were completely and fully developed. At that point others' and your own tolerance for your experimentation and errors decreased dramatically.

In my case, I seldom fit in the way my parents would have preferred. I was full of questions and challenges. Looking back, I realize that as a boy I was quite bright and rather immature at the same time. I was a bit of a late bloomer, which did not make a happy combination for my beleaguered father, who just wanted me to learn to mind. It also created problems for my mother, who was always trying to negotiate a truce without having to choose sides.

Continuing my instinctive pattern in a family with little tolerance for deviations, I flunked out of college, married early, returned and graduated from college, searched for a career that fit and settled on banking, eventually had two sons, divorced after a long time but when my boys were still quite young, raised them by myself and stayed in banking to provide stability for my family of three way longer than it was a good vocational fit for me. I knew what and who I didn't want to be much more clearly than who and what I wanted to be. I hadn't the confidence or tolerance for risk that would have allowed me to leave AND be a responsible single parent. I opted for security and stability. In the meantime, awaiting some unspecified form of personal enlightenment, I earned an MA in Counseling/ Vocational Rehabilitation because I thought I wanted to be a clinical psychologist, all the while raising kids and working full-time. It took a while. My life road had lots of twists and turns. Except for illegal substances, there wasn't much I didn't try.

I finally left The Bank of America and went to work for Right Management, an international outplacement/organizational consulting company. What I discovered in completing my first master's and, later, in leaving banking was that I was capable of blowing the lid off the box without first knowing exactly where I was going. I could successfully take some risks without unduly putting my sons at risk. I could have intentions, a partial plan, and invent and adapt the rest as I went along. It was liberating. And it was the beginning of my belief in lifelong human development and lifelong learning.

After several years I left the consulting organization and went out on my own. My boys grew up and, appropriately, began lives on their own. In response to their departure (kids leave and, I can say from personal experience, single parents, even if they are happy about the transition, are often left with a lot of empty, unfamiliar life space), I started looking for a community that was about professional and personal development. I discovered developmental psychology, the study of how we grow and change and acquire the new skills and knowledge we need across our life spans. I also discovered organizational psychology, the study of the components of how organizations succeed, stall, or fail. I embraced both developmental and organizational psychology and chose to study them. I earned a second MA (focused on learning and failure to learn in the workplace) and a PhD (my dissertation was focused on what types of social networks promote or obstruct which types of learning and vice versa, especially in the workplace).

All the while I continued working full-time in my own businesses.

I knew by then that I was unlikely to choose just one thing that would endure for the rest of my life. This meant I had to reconsider my identity (who I thought I was and how I knew) and create intentions for my life into which I poured a great amount of energy . . . all the while knowing I might have to revise my intentions as I went along. I had to surrender my impractical notions of finally arriving at a permanent and eternal destination. It isn't easy to joyously and doggedly pursue your intentions all the while not being overly attached to them because some of them might have to change significantly over time.

I also found the person with the right soul behind the eyes (my dominant requirement for a partner) and, eventually, after kissing herds of frogs, remarried. My wife is a force of nature and the brightest woman I know. Earlier in life, romance can often be about building a future that can include a home, babies, pets, and all of the other validators and expectations we've identified as our own version of the American Dream. It's my experience that, later in life, romance is often both much simpler and more complex than earlier. It's simpler because lots of our earlier needs have been met and we have fewer expectations of personal completion through a relationship. We've got a lot more life experience and, hopefully, a deeper sense of who we are and what we bring to a relationship without all the noise of so many things to do that we hardly know where to start. It's more complex because we're likely to be swept away and starry-eyed *but* we often have much more sophisticated expectations of intellectual parity, consistent openness and honesty, more demanding forms of mutual support that we have to create and deliver carefully because they come from who we have become, more than from the norms and expectations of others, and the need to work with the eccentricities, habits, and preferences that each partner has developed through the years. It's an opportunity for a higher quality of belonging than we earlier imagined existed.

In our case, we both wanted someone of "equal voltage" (well-matched power and ability albeit at different things perhaps), the kind of home base and support that would allow each of us to extend ourselves and do things we might not be able to pull off on our own, and the relief of freedom from gender-based—and therefore limiting—thinking about which of us was responsible for what and who was in control or in charge, and the ability to bring to each other the forms and abilities for play that each of us had developed through our own experiences and interests. After 18 years together in a later romance relationship, no matter how happy or unhappy we might be with each other or with ourselves in any given moment, we have the consistent ability to support and dance together literally and figuratively through whatever is in front of us.

I discovered the hard way that I sometimes had issues only therapy could address by diagnosing the condition, treating it, and working toward being "cured."

I also discovered the hard way that sometimes I had issues or was in situations that required assistance that didn't look like therapy. These issues and situations were changes right on schedule—however uncomfortable—and the only way out was through. These didn't require therapy at all. Nothing was wrong with me. The children grew up and left. My hair started turning gray and thinning. My mother and grandmother both died; the matriarchs and the structures and order they brought were gone. I became increasingly disenchanted with my banking work because what had begun as a great profession/person match had become a mismatch. I had gone one direction over time and the industry had gone another. Developmentally, I was exactly where I was supposed to be. These changes required me to step up, pay attention to what was really going on, and make responsible decisions. I began to see transitions as developmental and enlightening rather than only as problematic and tied to something for which I needed to seek a professional and a cure.

My sons are long since well established in their own lives. I now have seven (count them!) grandchildren. I have four businesses that involve a virtual staff. I'm not a candidate for a single job or label or solution or container in the workplace or at home. I'm partnered with a really interesting woman and we do interesting things. I like living the distributed or portfolio life.

What's the point of this story? In a segment of my professional life and in writing this book, I'm studying our transitions After 50 AND living it simultaneously and personally. I believe in lifelong development, not just the acquisition of information but true, deep development of the individual in response to and for what will be required by life and ambition tomorrow and in the future. I am one of the readers this book addresses. I am one of the students and teachers. I'm also an expert, a learner, a pioneer, a searcher, and a life colleague for each of my readers.

When I was young, age 50 sounded ancient. Fifteen years left to work. Ten golden years of pensioned leisure. Decline and death. That is one tenacious model. It doesn't want to admit it's no longer timely or accurate for many of us, and some of us don't want to admit it, either.

Now age 50 sounds young; it is a time to treasure the best of the past, letting go of what is no longer useful and looking forward to a lot of newness. We have many great years ahead, which may well be filled with some of the most creative and important work, relationships, and leisure activities of our lives. We are also living in a time of the greatest quantity and speed of change in human history. Keeping our wits about us and living a conscious life will be essential.

Our new "transitioning generation" of long-lived people After 50 has high expectations and the need to invent—and reinvent and financially support—their futures. We are them.

Today, as a consequence of the turbulent global economy, global warming, globalization through technologies, our transition from a manufacturing to a service economy, societal transformation, the likelihood of individual extended life spans, revolutions in political parties, purveyance of false news stories, and potential change in everything from supervision of banking to viewpoints on civil rights to how work for pay is configured, your life is unlikely to be as predictable or as permanent as it may have seemed in the past.

Let's look at the likelihood of predictability through the lens of longevity. People are living longer; the average life expectancy is now 77.5 years. Someone age 65 will live, on average, another 18.4 years. As individuals, will we all live longer? Probably not. As individuals, will many of us have an extended life span? Absolutely. This means we'll have a longer time to deal with unpredictability. It won't go away just because we have reached a certain age. We don't know the future impact of genome research on health care and longevity, but I expect it to be substantial and sooner than we think. In fact, genomic possibilities may be the new boom industry as digital has been until now.

Let's look at the likelihood of unpredictability through the lens of our working careers. Increasingly, people don't spend their entire career at one employer or in one line of work. Increasingly, companies we go to work for out of college eventually no longer exist or are nearly unrecognizable after a series of downsizings, consolidations, mergers, and acquisitions. Many of us who have lost our employment have had a series of part-time jobs or long periods of unemployment, which in turn means downsizing life-styles and expectations. People of all ages are becoming more entrepreneurial as technologies and freelancing permit a significant redistribution of work and compensation in comparison to a job being the only possibility. This means that the likelihood of unpredictability will be something we will have to recognize and work with for much longer in our careers and personal lives than we would have imagined earlier.

In my own life, I am choosing how to bring forward the most useful experiences and knowledge from my past regardless of how attached I am to what went on before. I am releasing with appreciation those parts that have served me well (and maybe not so well sometimes) in the past but may not be useful to me going forward. I don't want to totally reinvent myself as if nothing from the past was of value. Reinvention sounds good but, if we aren't careful, it also can force us to leave some of our most valuable skills, knowledge, and sense of ourselves by the side of the road. I also know that some of what worked for me in the past not only won't work in the future but could actually work against me. Why would I want to bring forward something from my past that could well work against me in my future? Habit? Laziness? Romantic attachment? Sounds like way too much work.

Nancy Collamer, a friend and colleague of mine, is the author of *Second-Act Careers: 50+ Ways to Profit from Your Passions During Semi-Retirement*. She is also a great professional advisor, speaker, coach, and regular contributor to NextAvenue.org (PBS site for people over 50), Forbes.com, and USNews.com. You can find her at http://www.mylifestylecareer.com.

■

OUR WIDE-RANGING INTERVIEW INCLUDED THIS QUESTION ON REINVENTION:

George: So what happens if you've been doing something for quite a while and you're kind of bored with it and there is a possibility that you could be learning something brand new? Is it OK to abandon what you've been historically good at?

Nancy: I think if you're ready to do what it takes to completely and totally reinvent yourself in a new field, then of course it's OK. BUT for as much as we talk about reinvention, the reality is most people don't really reinvent. What most people do is repurpose and recycle and repackage their skills in new and interesting ways. And they weave them together with new interests and new outlets, and, by doing that, they're able to build on the foundation that they already have. They're more able then to take on different types of projects and assignments and work that are much more interesting to them.

So, I think that the media loves—and having a media presence I totally get this—the stories about the attorney turned cattle rancher. In practicality that's really a tough road for most people to follow. What I say to people is, "Look, even if you really didn't like your job, spend some time analyzing and dissecting it to figure out the parts and pieces, the skills, projects, people, and environments that you did enjoy. Use those as a foundation to begin to build whatever is next. And by doing that you're able, rather than starting at Ground Zero, to take advantage of the experiences and connections of all those years of work. It just seems to me at age 60 to completely abandon the value and content of your experience without really thinking it through doesn't make sense. If you are ready to do it and if you are just crazy passionate about doing something else that meets your reasonable needs, then by all means go for it. But I think for most people it makes a lot more sense to at least begin with the foundation of deeply understanding the important pieces of your experience and then weaving in those other things that really interest you.

Careful, thoughtful, courageous selection of what to bring forward and what to leave behind is one of the hallmarks of our development After 50.

When I think of the years ahead, I have made a conscious decision to establish what I have dubbed my several ponies on the track of life. Each pony is a small business or my engagement with my children/grandchildren or my volunteer work or my time with my wife or creative pursuits or health-related activity or alone time (which I didn't used to enjoy and now consider to be essential). While each pony has its own identity, combined as a herd they represent a full life for me. Not one of them owns me completely. Hooray! All of them add to and complement my quality of life, which was the starting point. All of them demand attention, creativity, and a healthy me. They each give me energy and insight, which help me work with their fellow ponies. I keep my networks of important relationships vital and regularly renewed.

What does it take for us to pull all of this off? We need a fluid and adept combination of:

1. A high level of self-awareness
2. A high level of awareness of the world around us
3. Incremental planning
4. Inventing it as we go
5. Making great decisions about which new and incoming information to use and which to ignore (a selection not based on outdated preferences or habitual prejudices)
6. Adapting plans and ourselves as necessary to achieve a high quality of life as previous decisions/commitments are no longer appropriate and new questions arise

Much that we have taken for granted based on how our parents or grandparents lived has changed so dramatically that the old rules and assumptions are probably not applicable. How much sense does it make for us to remain untouched and unchanged when the many facets of the environment around us are changing rapidly?

Here are some examples of what has changed and will continue to do so in the coming years:

- The United States' position in the world.
- How long you're going to live.
- Available funds to use to pay for your longer life (Hint: It may not be pensions or Social Security even if you have them now.)
- Our assumption that retirement is a natural and highly desirable stage of life, the automatic outcome of years of work.
- Our increasing and profound need for extended stimulation, engagement, accomplishment, and meaning through much longer life spans.
- The strategic value, leverage, and future of a college education AND commitment to lifelong learning, beginning no later than the day you graduate.
- What retirement really looks like today, including how it is configured, adopted, and whether it is delayed.
- The shorter shelf life of knowledge and experience due to the accelerating rate of change all around us. Knowledge and wisdom are no longer necessarily an automatic function of having lived a long time. Age doesn't guarantee wisdom. Neither does youth. Lifelong learning is increasingly a reality and a necessity for a successful life.
- The increasing amount of technological knowledge required to do simple things like operating a car, playing "the stereo," setting the bedside table clock, or operating the toaster. This doesn't even count the array of smart tablets, clothing that tracks your activities, computer watches, and the ubiquitous cell "phone" as camera, communication device, financial access instrument, calendar, game center, and health-care access vehicle.

- Institutions including what we've called "traditional" marriage, the nuclear family, and the value and place of political parties.
- The role and duration of childhood.
- Work for pay configurations. Freelancing may well eclipse jobs in the future.

WHO SHOULD READ THIS BOOK AND WHY?

How are people—between age 50 and much older—going to navigate life's curvy and evolving highway with so much in flux? How can we get there from here when the old rules no longer apply?

These are vastly different times for this age group. And, at the risk of repeating some of what I've explained in the Introduction, I can't stress enough that this will not be a straight road for most of you. Your routes will change. Curves will suddenly emerge on straightaways. What you thought looked like a great job may disappear when your employer is sold. New software has just been installed that will take over some of the most interesting parts of the job you have been doing for a long time or dramatically alter the kinds of expertise you must have to succeed in the job.

Daniel J. Martin is a highly seasoned professional financial advisor in Pittsburgh who has watched and worked with many people struggling with their own relationships to retirement through the years. Dan can be contacted at http://www.monteverdegroup.com/Daniel-J--Martin,-RFC.e92229.htm.

When I interviewed Dan, we focused on his observations on the realities of retirement within his cohort.

George: Once people decide on what retirement should look like for them—financially, vocationally, and personally—is it likely to change?

Dan: Oh, yes! I have several physicians who had planned on retiring maybe in their late 50s or early 60s. Sixtyish. Just due to basic burnout and the fact that physician compensation isn't what it used to be. Not by a long shot. These are people who are now exploring ways of continuing to work at least part-time—you know, maybe do an emergency medical clinic kind of thing, just to pick up a shift here and there, just to generate some cash. But probably more important—and once again this probably dovetails into your work—is that people have discovered that retirement is, the dog who catches the bumper of the car. Now that you've got it, what are you going to do with it?

George: [laughter]

Dan: I mean, I can't tell you how many people I have who are really bad at retirement. The irony is that many of the people who are most financially capable of retiring and not working are the ones who do it least well. The ones who have saved, and are highly successful, and could walk away at any time without ever looking back, are the ones who hold on forever, in many cases, as long as possible, simply because psychologically they can't get their arms around the fact that nobody cares what they think anymore.

George: Is there an inverse correlation, at least to some degree, between financial success and the ability to retire successfully?

Dan: Exactly. Exactly. My most successful clients are the ones who in some way, shape, or form will work till they drop. And if they can't find something in their own career, they're going to go buy a business or something to play with. Only because they need some reason to get up in the morning. And those of us who live in the Northeast are . . . you know, every day you can't play golf, every day you can't drive your convertible. And even if you could, who would you drive it with?

George: Are you saying successful retirement means becoming someone you haven't been?

Dan: Sometimes. How can you change your life that much by no longer working and not have to change yourself?

Your destinations may disappear while you're on the way somewhere. What seemed an ultimate career goal when you graduated from college either doesn't exist anymore or looks far less interesting to the more experienced you than it used to look. The man or woman you couldn't wait to marry may want different things than you want 30 years later. Signs won't necessarily be there at all or, if they are, you may not immediately know which to read and rely on. Curve Ahead may not appear in your consciousness. Instead, in a Lightbulb moment, you may see a Curve Just Passed in your rearview mirror. And you will have to adapt accordingly.

Welcome to the new normal of many anticipated and unanticipated curves and straightaways. Welcome to needing to distinguish between continuous and discontinuous change in order to react and adapt accordingly.

The primary readers for this book are individuals between age 50 and much older, people who are likely to have more, not fewer, surprise curves on their life roadways as time passes. Why age 50? It's arbitrary, I admit. Fifty is frequently around the time when there is a tectonic shift in your relationships with your children, work, dreams, yourself, and your ambitions/intentions. Why not wait until much later in life to pay attention to this? Because many people now have a much longer runway than anyone expected. You could be one of them. You may have planned and saved, expecting to live to age 84. In fact, many of us will live longer with very high levels of vitality and equally high expectations for engagement, stimulation, and contribution.

Not all of us will, of course, but if you or your spouse turns out to live to age 96, for instance, instead of age 84, what will a high-quality, sustainable life look like during the extra 12 years? How will you create it for yourselves? It probably won't be through the endless leisure or the old retirement models. How will you pay for it? Who will you want and need to be your companions during these years? How will your own needs and priorities change? They are as unlikely to remain unchanged as you are yourself.

As Americans, many of us pay a lot of attention to senior and elderly services. We want the "elderly or senior years" to be high quality.

In my opinion we correspondingly fail to pay enough attention to the developmental runway of life and the years that precede late life beginning at around age 50. Too many of us are limiting our attention to retirement and other stale, dated constructs instead of looking at our own development after 50, which includes but is certainly not limited to retirement as it used to be. This book is my effort to begin to shift our attention to learning and a high quality of life that may well occur in our later years. However, the ability to lead a satisfying, happy, and healthy existence when you're 90 doesn't start at age 88. It must begin years earlier than that.

The word *retirement* is, of course, problematic. It suggests permanent surrender of work in favor of permanent leisure. Retirement for each of us can be different because it's so personal. I think Bobbie's "retirement story" is more common than we think in its continuation of life and in the individuality of how it plays out. It's the story of a life roadway we call retirement that is actually the continued living of a life with less paid work than before but with lots of intentions, surprises, and adaptation.

THE RETIREMENT STORY OF BOBBIE, AGE 67

I was born and raised in Panama. I am an American. My parents were American, too. My mother was an Army nurse and my father was an Army doctor. They were stationed in Panama in WWII. They met when a friend of my father's was sick and my father, visiting him, met his charming young nurse who turned out to be my mother. My father started going back daily. Romantic! They stayed in Panama and built a life together, eventually with me and my sister. The only time I ever left there was to come up to the States to go to college and university and then right back. So that's the only life I had ever lived.

My retirement had to do with the signing of the Panama Canal Treaty, and the stipulation that all of the resident American citizens had to leave what is now the former canal zone by Dec. 31, 1999, and you know, no one could have foreseen that coming. I worked for the U.S. Dept. of Defense as an elementary school principal, K–6.

I thought at full but early retirement I could come up here to the States and live with my mother and father because they were elderly and I could help out in that way. So I was in the right place at the right time. I came up here and I bought this house and moved my mom and dad in with me, and ended up being their caretaker for five years. I wouldn't give that up for anything. But it was bookends to the other end of life . . . you know. How they were so wonderful to me when I was a kid; I mean they gave my sister and me a really great life. For me it was difficult, but it was an actual privilege and I—as odd as it sounds—I would probably give everything I have for one more day of it. It was 24-7. It's what I did and who I was.

When I moved to the U.S. even as a lifelong American citizen, it was such a huge transition. I went from speaking Spanish primarily to primarily English, and different food, different clothing, different money—from having people work for me at my home to being the equivalent of the maid for my parents and doing it all.

My husband passed away; I went from having a big job to no job, lots of friends to knowing nobody. I mean it was just like—it was huge—and then, I forgot, the icing on the cake—after my parents moved in with me and my mother started having strokes and getting really mean, I discovered a lump, and it turned out I had breast cancer.

I just kept thinking about that. "Well, this is it. This is my time. I can sink or I can swim. I gotta go." I would say I did it one day at a time. One step at a time. That's how you get through chemotherapy. You know, it's just like—that's what you do, and I had—all this was going on while I was recovering from the cancer, and having chemo and all of this—it just was literally one day at a time. Serendipity.

I had a neighbor who lived right next door to me, and he was a director at a local theater. I'd been living here about five years and my parents were approaching the end of their lives. One day he came over and knocked on the door and said that he was directing a play and he didn't have prop people. He needed people to move props backstage, and he knew that I was in here with nothing to do, and that I didn't ever go anywhere at night and it was time for me to get out and he said it would fulfill two things: It would help him and it would get me out of the house, and I just looked at him, and thought, "Well, this is just crazy enough. I'm going to do it!" So I did it. I went out and started propping, and I thought it was a lot of fun, and I met people and showbiz people are as a rule very odd and very fun and I was in a mood for that. I hadn't been around fun for a very long time. So the fun part definitely appealed to me. And that I was organized and a hard worker appealed to them. So from props, I got invited to move up into the booth and learn the sound computer and start working the sound. And then from there I got invited to work on the other side, to do the lights, so I learned that. And then I started getting invited to be the stage manager. That's the person right under the director. And so then I was in charge of all of it. So that's what I've been doing now. I'm pretty much stage manager.

I was thinking that a good analogy for me would be that my life has been like a play. Like a three-act play, and you know, there are many scenes—there could be many scenes within an act. But the first act would be being born and childhood and young adulthood and going to school and so forth and so on, and the second act would be then young adulthood, getting that first job, if you're lucky finding a mate and having a family and so forth and so on, and then I think act three would be retirement, and the final part of that life, and the third part of that life, and that's where I am. I'm in act three and I'm just having the best time. Turns out it's not bad! I'm having a lovely act three. I would wish it on everybody. It's been so much about me living my life and so comparatively little about my retirement. I would hope everybody would get this.

Bobbie's's story is not dominated by her retirement. What stands out is that she continued living her life.

Back to Who Should Read This Book

The secondary audience are readers between ages 15 and 50. Why these ages? From a human development perspective, those are years in which you're continually doing the work to be a great 18- or 37- or 33- or 45-year-old. However, a great 18-year-old doesn't start at age 17. Opportunities, obstacles, and more accumulate over your life. What did we used to be great at that no longer serves us well? What are we going to have to be great at instead? What new and cataclysmic changes in our work or personal lives render what we used to be good at absolutely obsolete?

These change catalysts can vary from peak experiences, like completing graduate school or backpacking in Nepal or winning a major sports competition, to bottoming-out experiences, like what it takes to finally get to Alcoholics Anonymous or bankruptcy, divorce, or job loss, often only to discover you're eventually much better off and happier in your new work or situation than you were in your old one. We're never fully formed until our bodies stop for the last time. And then, who knows?

If you are a parent or grandparent, you can use this book to teach your kids and grandchildren more effective thinking and practical life skills that are necessary in today's evolving world. You can create developmental experiences for and with them (e.g., a tour of a local museum or business or a trip to another climate or topography or society) that will add to their usable knowledge and challenge their assumptions. (CAUTION: Never try to teach or push something you haven't done or aren't willing to do for the first time yourself.) Teenagers—especially given today's technologies—are very knowledgeable and capable. They are also often into continual multitasking. How sweet would it be to take them somewhere they haven't been, to have an experience they haven't had, that will open new roadways regarding people, places, and possibilities? No cell phones or tablets for two days at least. My own example: My oldest granddaughter, then age 14, wanted to go to Marine Biology Summer Camp as a certified scuba diver. Since I was sending her to the camp, I offered to pay for her PADI scuba training. "Only if we do it together," she said. We became the granddaughter/grandfather dive team that became PADI Open Water Dive Certified together. A developmental, new experience for each of us complete with new people, perspectives, experiences, and budding memories.

It can work in reverse, too. We can learn from our kids and grandkids. I recently took my five oldest grandchildren (ages 7 to 16) to a movie (they got to choose), then to dinner, and finally for ice cream. I was driving my daughter-in-law's large Mom van, a developmental experience for me all the way around. Have you ever tried to park one of those vans full of kids in a crowded movie theater parking lot with people watching you? We saw *Big Hero 6*, had restaurant pasta (the kids got to choose the restaurant), and only a few of us could finish our ice cream at Cold Stone. I was one of those who could not.

I gave them a movie, dinner, dessert, and time as a group with me. This has become a regular event for all of us. They give me another peek into their thinking and their futures. And they teach and mentor me. Have you ever had your teenage granddaughter look you in the eye and say, "Tell us what you really thought of the movie, Poppa. We know when you're just humoring us"? They thought we saw an engaging movie in *Big Hero 6*. I thought we saw an allegory that powerfully opened STEM learning (science, technology, engineering, math) as pathways for kids to desirable passions and future careers, complete with animated movie role models. The kids and the experience taught me, yet again, that the more I know, the more aware I am of how much I don't know. And I've grown to like it that way.

We're drowning in information being pushed at us through technologies and specialized professional service providers, but we're often uncertain about what information to trust and what to discard. If you aren't feeling overloaded with data from multiple, especially digital, sources, you may not be paying close enough attention.

All of us are being tracked, studied, predicted, and sold to through technologies and data, big and small. This is happening through the foggy prevalence of fear-based content and fearmongering, high levels of social/belief polarization, and omnipresent pill-like lists of the five action steps for this and the seven things to know about that.

This book is a practical navigation guide for you and the journey you're on for the rest of your life. You can do some planning and also invent your route as you go. But you must start paying close attention. It will serve you well to create priorities, sort information, and build adaptable plans that are right for you. Change will happen with and without your permission, plan or no plan. That's where agility and paying attention come in. Life usually requires both.

While you can no longer rely exclusively on earlier rules and signs, your journey may also be filled with greater opportunities than you ever expected.

chapter 3

A Tour of the New Normal

G iven the increasing pace of change, it's more important than ever to create the right mix of planning and action. And it's trickier than it has been for earlier generations. It has been kind and generous of others—parents, friends, people we observe or hear about but don't know, the media—however deliberately or inadvertently—to do some developmental pioneering for us. We've learned by observing how they raised their children, did their work and got promoted (or didn't), treated their friends, planned (or didn't) in collaboration with their spouses, made (and didn't) their financial and social decisions, and how they regarded their own aging after age 50. Sometimes we have paid close attention. Other times we've ignored them and their experience altogether. What have we learned from our parents, siblings, coworkers, and friends' successes and mistakes? What have we learned from our own experience? What have we done with that insight as well as insight about ourselves? Cultivating that learning—which applies in the short term but is unlikely to last forever—those insights are an essential part of our lifelong development because they so deeply inform our beliefs, behaviors, imagination, and options, provided we're paying attention.

I see Fred Mandell of Needham, Massachusetts, as a Renaissance Man. Fred's mission is to help individuals, leaders, and their teams unlock their full creative powers. As CEO of The Global Institute for the Arts and Leadership (TGIAL), he has mobilized a worldwide network of artists, leaders, entrepreneurs, academics, researchers, and consultants who believe in the power of the arts to lead positive transformational change in our organizations and society. A CEO, an artist, a PhD in history, and an organizational consultant, Fred can be reached through www.artschangeleaders.org.

There is, I can tell you from personal experience, no end to the interesting topics one can discuss with Fred. When I interviewed him, we tried to focus on what's different now and the accompanying realities.

George: What are we facing today?

Fred: If we look at the world today, it's very different in dramatic ways from 15 to 20 years ago. And it's different because the speed of change, the disruptive nature of change, all kinds of things are going on which introduce a very different set of dynamics than existed previously where the world, even if we didn't realize it at the time, was on a more gradual trajectory. And now we open a newspaper [and], see political change threatening at our doorsteps; we see economic change highly disruptive in terms of 2008. So this is all a boiling stew, and I think it requires a more heightened sense of creative sensibilities for people to be able to make sense of that. Today, not only are we living longer, but we are living longer in a more destabilized context. You and I know that we want to banish the word "retirement" and, if we're successful in doing that, we've introduced a new set of motivations on the part of folks who are aging and want to be engaged. But how does one get engaged in this new context in ways that enable them to make a meaningful contribution rather than creating fear and paralysis?

It's nice to know we have much in common with others. Still, in the end, it's called my (or your) life for a reason. We're similar but also unique. No one else is inside our skin. No one can or should take more responsibility for our lives than we do. That's what being a grown-up is all about, and it's very demanding when done well.

WHY CAN'T I JUST LEAP INTO ACTION?

Planning and action are each important. In the right amounts and at the right times, linked together, they will deliver success.

What do we hope to get from planning? First, you get clarity about your direction and intentions. Second, there is decreased (but not eliminated) risk. Third, there is greater confidence from being organized. Fourth, there is the discovery of potentially better alternatives. Fifth, a greater likelihood of success through a combination of achievement and smart adapting as time passes and new information becomes available. This all presumes, of course, that you regularly review and update your plan. If you don't, a plan can rapidly become the equivalent of an outdated, unconsulted road map stashed in the dashboard's glove box.

What do we hope to get from action? First, there is immediate gratification that comes from motion and momentum. Second, you get progress and a sense of accomplishment. Third, you get important requested and unrequested feedback and insight. Fourth, there is a decrease in anxiety that waiting—even well informed waiting—can produce. Don't underestimate our capacity for leaping into action as an anxiety-reduction tool. Consider the attendant cost in time, resources, and energy. Action from habit or for its own sake may not be a great investment. Remember to do a reality check periodically. How well informed is your action? How well informed can it be?

TOO MUCH ACTION, TOO LITTLE PLANNING

Sam and Norma left the freezing temperatures of Cincinnati and fled on holiday to coastal Florida one recent January. Upon arrival, they found the weather to be perfect. They loved walking on the beach in the sunshine holding hands. They enjoyed the restaurants, cultural events, and interesting sites. They found the other snowbirds at adjacent tables to be fun to talk to. They loved being outdoors, golfing, and biking. In short, they fell in love with the place. In one giant, spontaneous leap, they agreed they had found the perfect place to live. No more ice. No more snow. Since both were eligible for early retirement, it seemed simple. They both intended to get part-time jobs after moving. They bought a new house in a Florida retirement community, went back to Cincinnati, did take early retirement, told their kids and grandkids they were moving, sold their house, and made the move. By April they were settled in their new Florida location. It was heaven for about three months.

By the end of May, the newness was beginning to wear off. They found living in a retirement community far less stimulating than they expected, particularly when they discovered that many of the residents were snowbirds and part-time residents. Sam and Norma lived on a street where fewer than half the houses were occupied year-round. The Florida temperatures and humidity began to soar. Interesting part-time jobs were much harder to find than they expected. Volunteer positions were plentiful with the many local nonprofits. They began to miss their grandkids but discovered that—since the kids were getting older now and no longer babies—they and their parents had significant school and sports commitments, which made them unavailable except at holidays and during summer vacation.

Two years later, Sam and Norma sold their Florida house and moved back to Cincinnati. They bought a house down the street from their old one. They also bought a Florida timeshare where they expect to spend the month of January every year. They are in the process of looking for part-time jobs and they are seeing a lot of their grandkids.

TOO MUCH PLANNING, TOO LITTLE ACTION

Beth and Mark wanted an SUV to pull their 20-foot boat. They loved to fish. They loved to be together on the water. They loved to try out different lakes and explore in their boat.

They divided up the duties. Mark would do research on the SUV. Beth would do research on the best loan packages. Their approach was similar: They used spreadsheets to identify the major products (SUVs in Mark's case and loan programs in Beth's) down the left column. Across the top, in Mark's case, were brand, number of doors, amount of horsepower and tow capability, transmission options, cost to insure, price of the trailer license, how much he liked the dealer's salesperson, and 16 other discrete SUV criteria. Across the top, in Beth's case, were down payment/equity required, interest rate, number of months and years allowed, monthly payment, how much she liked the bank's lending officer, and 22 other criteria that she thought were important.

All of the information went into Microsoft Project software on their computer at home for the ease of updating and data massage.

They began the Boat Project in late August. By the time they completed the data gathering and investigation, it was late October. The new year's models were out. Mark and Beth definitely wanted the newest model. They hadn't bought that many cars in their life together and both wanted the other to have a brand-new car. So, using the new year's models, they began the data collection all over again. Then Thanksgiving and Christmas arrived.

The following March, Mark's employer eliminated many jobs and instituted layoffs. Mark lost his position, but he was fortunate. Within six months, he was back at work. The couple needed to replenish their savings account, and they took four months to do it. Then they went SUV shopping again. Once again the new models were out. Once again they began their data collection.

They think this year will be the year of the new SUV for them. All their friends certainly hope so.

These are two different approaches actually taken by two couples. If we need to create the right amount of planning and the right amount of action, what's a great model for doing that? While there isn't a universal, perfect answer to that question because circumstances vary so widely, this is a model that works very well.

The shelf life of education, knowledge, and experience is growing ever shorter. This means adopting the life habit of really smart research and inquiry. The quality of the question drives the quality of the answer.

One tool used by professional advisors—psychologists, attorneys, HR professionals—is known as a Learning and Decision Making Loop. (See Figure 3-1.) You begin with an event and work your way around the loop, arriving at a comparable event in the future with a different, more informed viewpoint. These learning loops can be cumulative, in effect stacked upon each other. When imagined this way and seen from the side, the learning loops cumulatively form an upward learning spiral.

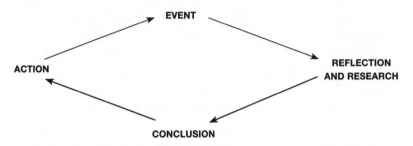

Figure 3-1. Learning and Decision Making Loop.

MY OWN EXAMPLE

Event: In our late 50s, my wife and I concluded that the large city where we were living was unlikely to be a great place for us to grow older and we would be better off if we made a well-informed leap while we were still young enough to return if our choice turned out to be a disaster. Neither of us had any desire to retire (as in not working at all) . . . and we still haven't. We had made an agreement that we would try it—whatever it turned out to be—for five years. If it wasn't a successful experiment, we could return to where we started. We didn't sell our city condo; we rented it out instead. Whether or not our choice proved sound, we would have the confidence and experience of trying and knowledge about ourselves that would serve us well for the rest of our lives individually and as a couple. It was my job to go out and get the data. I couldn't come to a conclusion or make any commitments without the full involvement of both of us.

Research: We used a combination of a Template of Needs and On-site Interviews to discover major possibilities for ourselves.

Template of Needs (in random order):

1. A great, warm climate for me and a balm for my life-long eczema/atopic dermatitis
2. Near the ocean
3. Universities in the area
4. Friendly to small businesses
5. Lots of arts and politics
6. Other people/couples taking risks and trying on new lives
7. A major airport within an hour
8. A house we love or like very much
9. Topography and weather that would make regular outdoor exercise much more likely for both of us than our prior windy and hilly city had been
10. Reasonably affordable
11. Great local health care

On a scale of 1 to 10, we rated each component of the Template of Needs at every location we visited.

We knew that we were unlikely to find a place with a high score in all the categories and agreed we would work with resulting trade-offs as we went along.

Whom did we interview? What did we ask?

You will often hear me say that the quality of the question drives the quality of the answer. I think "When can I retire?" is a bozo question because it is just too simplistic. In fact, in my opinion, one of the greatest After 50 skills is asking more and much smarter questions than we did earlier in our lives.

My wife and I identified the places that were most likely to score high on our template. Before leaping into action, I contacted a variety of friends and asked, "Who do you know who lives in Austin or San Diego or Phoenix or Charleston or any of the other places on our list? Who has moved there recently? Would you open the door for me to talk with them in person when I'm visiting their area?" Everywhere I went

I not only saw realtors and talked to the Chamber of Commerce, I also invited a friend of a friend to dinner to ask questions:

1. Now that you've been here for a while, how good a choice has it proven to be?
2. How did you choose it to begin with?
3. What has come as a pleasant surprise?
4. What have you had to learn the hard way that you wish you had known in advance?
5. If you had it to do all over again, what would you do? Differently? The same?
6. What has been the easiest part of assimilating here?
7. What has been the most difficult part of assimilating here?
8. What have you discovered about yourself here that you didn't know before?
9. What is missing that you wish you had? What is in excess here?
10. What am I not asking you about that's important for me to know?

CONCLUSION

After each trip—the data collection took about two years—my wife and I would return from a trip with information. We would review the information together. In the end, it was coming down to the Phoenix area and we thought we could occasionally visit an ocean. Trade-offs again!

Our live roadways have straightaways. They also have hairpin turns. Less and less is orderly, slow, and linear. Frequently we can't see around the corner. What you are looking for may come from well outside your intentions and efforts. Be prepared to remain open and aware.

Then my wife and I were sitting in a great big-city tapas restaurant, just the two of us, reviewing the interview data, talking about the template, and comparing notes. The couple at the next table began, unnoticed, to eavesdrop. Finally, they interrupted our conversation, saying, "We've been looking, too. Like you, we've been here for years. Unlike you, we weren't organized about our search. We did, however, luck into finding a place that meets all of your template's requirements. In fact, we just bought a condo there. Would you like the name and number of our realtor? It's Sarasota, Florida."

"Florida?" I asked? "We went to the East Coast of Florida and it didn't much match our template." "No," they answered. "You weren't listening. We said Sarasota. It's to Florida what Austin is to Texas without the state buildings."

The couple wrote the realtor's name and phone number on a cocktail napkin, I put it in my pocket, thanked them for the information. We've never seen them since.

Eventually, my wife and I agreed, life had intervened and hit us over the head with one more possibility. We decided we needed to delay our decision one more time. I called my friends again and asked if they knew anyone in the Sarasota area. My friend Walt in Tahoe said his former competitor in the (I kid you not) coffin business in Ohio, Dennis, had retired there. Walt opened the door for me to visit Sarasota, meet Dennis, and ask all my questions.

It turned out that for us Sarasota had the highest score on our template of all the options we researched. We didn't want to be snowbirds. We didn't want endless leisure. We wanted to make the commitment of buying a house and living there full-time for five years. Would our experiment succeed? Would we gain the confidence and conscious awareness/competence that should result from living our way into the choice and risk?

Here we are nine years later. It wasn't always easy. It was often surprisingly challenging and rewarding. Our experiment has been a success. We aren't quite the same people as we were before. We have the security of knowing that no matter what happens through the rest of our lives, individually and as a couple, we have the ability individually and together to adapt, learn, enjoy, and prosper. That's no small ROI from the risk we took. Is this a good choice for everyone? No. But it surely worked for us. And your own large or small version of your own over-50 adventure could work for you.

We went around the learning loop countless times. An event would be imposed on us or we would seek an experience (an event), ask good questions (research), come to some sort of interim conclusion that would inform our action until the next time around the loop, which was usually sooner rather than later and informed our experience, research, and conclusion yet again.

ONE MORE LOOK AT THE LEARNING LOOP FROM A DIFFERENT PERSPECTIVE

Scale is very important. Are we seeing only single events or trips around the loop? Are we seeing several loops accrued over time, which form patterns? Are we seeing ourselves? Are we seeing impact on the loops of the larger systems in which we operate? Are we confusing—and overreacting to—single events, interpreting them as if they were patterns? Do we have the ability to know how far from something to stand to really see it? Or how close? Using scale effectively is an important After 50 skill. Therefore, it's important to see the learning loop as a single experience and as a series of experiences, connected and stacked upon each other, that establish one or more patterns that we can work with in our own learning. See Figure 3-2 below.

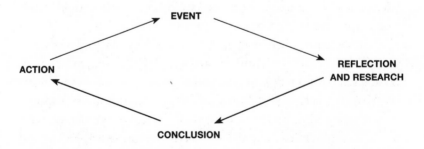

Figure 3-2.

One time around the Learning Loop is a smart thing to do. Cumulative, deliberate learning is even smarter.

Living your After 50 life with this model as a way of life can create the kinds of awareness, information gathering, informed conclusions and decisions, and smart actions that will be necessary After 50, as circumstances and we ourselves change with and without warning and with or without our permission. It sets up a continuous feedback loop, allowing you to make informed decisions and adjustments as you go along. Of course, this will call into question what is "normal" when life is lived based on change and a series of small and large course corrections as opposed to hanging onto one image or construct of "normal" for a long time.

A LOOK AT NEW NORMAL VS. OLD NORMAL

What role does "normal" play for many of us? We think of it as a rule or standard of behavior shared by members of our social group. We can trust it. It won't sneak up on us or make us look foolish. Norms may be internalized; they can be incorporated within the individual so that there is conformity without external rewards or punishments, or they may be enforced by positive or negative sanctions from without. The social unit sharing particular norms may be small (e.g., a clique of friends) or may include all adult members of a society. Norms are more specific than values or ideals: Honesty is a general value, but the cluster of rules and behaviors defining what constitutes honest behavior in a particular situation are norms.

Norms are usually paradoxical in nature. They are a kind of anchor to keep us from drifting too far. They can also serve to keep us anchored in place when we should be moving on:

1. They keep us safely and securely in place and comfortable regardless of what is happening around us. They also prevent us from moving and changing too quickly but also help us do so when it's necessary.
2. They keep us moving along; we can't stop and examine everything or we'd never get anything done. Also, they

often serve as a substitute for the work of thinking and questioning at important times because it's much easier to stay in Old Normal than it is to do the demanding, reflective work of reassessing its current validity.

3. They give us a strong decision-making framework and they regularly blind us through the illusion that there are no grays and only two alternatives, yes or no, black or white.

We naturally look for opposites to help us make sense of everything in between. And, again paradoxically, working only with opposites dramatically limits possibilities because everything in between is missed or dismissed. We use opposites as a basis for communication, too. It's how our bodies and brains are built. Opposites are comforting and don't require us to work hard at thinking, understanding, and deciding. Not one of these opposites would exist without the other. Black and white. Left and right. Up and down. Hot and cold. Light and dark. Dry and wet. Sharp and dull. Summer and winter. Back and forth. Try imagining morning without evening. They are both required.

This works so well for us, we use opposites to work with much more abstract concepts: Right and wrong. Young and old. Conservative and liberal. Progress and regress. Happy and unhappy. Normal and abnormal. Where we get into trouble is when we fail to acknowledge that there is any position or content between them that could possibly be equally valid or of value.

The truth about normal is that it is continually evolving. We also confuse normal with healthy (vs. unhealthy), moral (vs. immoral), or trustworthy (vs. untrustworthy). Every time we load these other dimensions onto normal, we charge the conversation and decrease the likelihood of successful communication. We may want to see normal as a fixed point—old or new—but that's more about our comfort, and sometimes intellectual laziness, than it is about truth. Some of what used to be normal is still normal: aging, working, procreation, enthusiasm, and disappointment,

New Normal is a term in business and economics that began with the financial conditions following the financial crisis of 2007–2008 and the aftermath of the 2008–2012 global recession.

The term has since been applied in a variety of contexts including social science. It suggests that what was previously abnormal has to be reexamined in the current context and often admitted into the normal category. There is no doubt that what was considered abnormal before may have since become commonplace. Living much longer. Much-reduced desire to retire. Gay marriage. Congressional polarization. Genetically altered foods. One truth about the new, technologically driven New Normal is that it will be both fast paced and include more than simple opposites.

The New Normal won't necessarily be a smooth extension of our past, adjusted for age and updated intentions. Intentions are expectations that are too distant or unformed to work well as a goal. If you have any doubts about this, go back to Chapter 2 and reread The Retirement Story of Bobbie. Yours probably won't be identical but it may have some of the same aspects.

Under the New Normal, each generation has the opportunity to learn from each of the others—from people both older and younger than they are. No single generation can know it all.

Dan Schawbel, himself a Millennial, is a *New York Times* best-selling author, serial entrepreneur, Fortune 500 consultant, Millennial TV personality, global keynote speaker, career and workplace expert, personal branding coach, and start-up advisor. His mission in life is to support his Millennial generation from student to CEO. I had the opportunity to interview Dan about the importance of goals and what shouldn't be a goal. You can learn more about Dan and his work at http://danschawbel.com.

George: How far out are your goals, Dan?

Dan: So here is what I do. I have five main business goals and five personal goals. For each goal I have a checklist with sub-goals and due dates. Some are pretty constant. Some are a little volatile. I've blown my goals away last year and this year. But I think I need at least 10 goals from a platform-building and financial standpoint to be relevant. But I've realized there are certain things I won't identify as a goal. I have a production company that's shopping around for a reality TV show. That was a goal last year but it's so unpredictable that it's not a goal for this year even though it's still in motion. I've learned what I can be accountable for and what is so out of my control that I can't really have a goal around it. I think you called those intentions earlier in our conversation, George.

Old Normal is a term developed from our increasing use of and embrace of the term New Normal. We needed an opposite to feel comfortable. There's the opposite theme again.

My colleague Richard Eisenberg is the managing editor and senior editor of the Money & Security and Work & Purpose channels at www.nextavenue.org (PBS Site for People 50 And Older). He has been a personal finance editor and writer at *Money*, Yahoo, *Good Housekeeping*, and CBS MoneyWatch. Rich can be reached through http://www.nextavenue.org/writer/richard-eisenberg.

When I interviewed Rich, we talked about aspects of what will compel us to change.

George: So what's going to be compelling to people in your opinion to begin to pay attention? Because our brains look for patterns and the familiar, a lot of these things are going to be unfamiliar unless we get the word out there. What's going to be compelling for people?

Rich: I think that what's going to be compelling is they know that the predictable life that they've led for the first, let's say, two or three decades of their working lives is ending or it has already ended. They know that it's going to be up to them to figure out how to deal with that, and if they don't, they realize that they could be depressed, they could be having serious financial problems, or they could be having serious relationship problems. So I think what's compelling them is they realize that basically they have no alternative but to figure it out on their own because they can't expect that things will just, you know, row along merrily the way they might have in the past. The pressure is on them.

George: And is that partly because our institutions—whether an employee pension system or the larger churches—will be unable to take care of us the way we used to expect?

Rich: I think it has a lot to do with the fact that the institutions have changed on us and we weren't necessarily prepared for that. Some of that change is from the employers and some of that, as you say, are really the changes in the accelerating load facing community organizations. Also, I think it has to do with families today and the fact that more of us are in a position where we need to do caregiving duties for our parents or our wives or husbands or relatives, brothers and sisters, in a way that maybe wasn't necessarily the case in the past, probably because fewer were living longer lives as they are today. Also, change has probably happened because the governments aren't providing for these kinds of things. So I think people will realize they have to come up with some ways to plan for these caregiving duties both in terms of geography—the ability to be there when the parent needs them—and being able to assume financial responsibility. And I think similarly the flip side is in many cases people in their 50s and 60s have adult children now and have very good relationships with their adult children. In the past, families tended to mostly stay in the same area all throughout their lives. These days, in many cases, the adult children have moved away because that's where their jobs are or because of a better fit for the life that they wanted to lead. This is not because they want to be away from their parents but because that's just where life is taking them. Now the 50-and-older parents are often finding that they want to come up with a solution to get closer one way or the other. This is and will be a compelling need.

It is important for people to see and think beyond the limits of the current "normal" because, unless we are careful, we tend to construct Old Normal as natural and good and construct New Normal as deviant and terrible. Do we do this because we are clinging to the familiar? Do we do this because we haven't paid enough attention to our evolution to see where the change is coming from? Try wading into the middle of the Colorado River at its silent but most powerful point above the dams. Hold your right hand out and try to stop the river. Then complain about the result. It seems to me we have to work with the river, not regret that we couldn't stop it. The same goes for the evolution of normal that is happening every day in large and small ways. Old Normal keeps changing. New

Normal keeps evolving. The pace accelerates. Real/current normal is what exists today. After 50 we won't be able to remain fixed points either and still be relevant.

What's a better way, then, to frame and understand what we are facing After 50 than Old and New Normal?

The answer is: growing our understanding and sophistication about change.

My colleague Kerry Hannon is a nationally recognized expert on career transitions, personal finance, and retirement. She is a frequent TV and radio commentator and is a sought-after keynote speaker at conferences across the country. She has spent more than two decades covering all aspects of careers, business, and personal finance as a columnist, editor, and writer for the nation's leading media companies, including the *New York Times*, *Forbes*, *Money*, *U.S. News & World Report*, and *USA Today*. (Find Kerry at www.kerryhannon.com.)

Part of our interview for the book focused on the impact of all of this change on women.

George: I'm looking at the numbers on late-in-life divorce and that's one of the fastest-growing rates of divorce. What does this mean for women?

Kerry: As you have probably heard, gray divorce is pretty common these days. And women who find themselves facing a split in their 50s and beyond need to cast a steely eye and get tough. This is not a time to fall apart and get strung out on emotional energy. It's business. Marriage, after all, at the core, is a business partnership.

One of the biggest mistakes women make is trying to cling to some symbol of security and stability amidst all the chaos. Emotionally, they want to hang on to the house in a divorce settlement. Rarely should you choose the house over retirement assets. The best scenario is to sell the house and split the proceeds.

Here's why: The retirement savings amassed by your spouse may be substantial and likely to grow in the future. But a home is probably going to cost you money to maintain and its future value is less predictable.

I advise women to negotiate hard for a portion of an ex's retirement assets, too, over alimony, if possible, because alimony is taxable and that's just a short-term plan. And if you are age 62 or older, were married for more than 10 years and have not remarried, you can claim on his Social Security. Collecting this benefit will not impact what your ex-spouse receives. Many women don't grasp these financial moves. It can help to have a certified financial planner at your side to help clear your head and get down to the brass financial tacks.

But, George, let's step back and look at the basic issues women face and why divorce trips them up financially in a far more painful way than it does their ex. Women are more likely to step away from their career paths by taking time off to raise children or care for aging parents. Men, on average, are in the workforce nine years longer than women, according to the Social Security Administration data.

Women also tend to work for smaller firms and nonprofits that either don't offer retirement savings plans or don't match employees' contributions to their retirement savings plans.

Then, too, yep, there's that nagging pay gap. Even professional women are earning 72 cents on the dollar to their male counterpart, according to the U.S. Census Bureau.

Finally, women also live on average five years longer than men. The truth is that most American women will find themselves single at some point from the age of 65 to the end of life. That means they don't have someone to share the cost of daily living expenses or to help with retirement savings.

Little wonder that study after study shows that after losing a partner due to death or divorce, a woman's standard of living generally drops. Barring large sums in life insurance or other assets, the economics of widowhood usually include a sharp drop in income, according to a report by the Women's Institute for a Secure Retirement, a nonprofit based in Washington, D.C. For many women, the road to poverty begins after their husbands die. As women age, they become more vulnerable to poverty. Nearly a third of single women over age 75 are living in poverty with less than $890 a month to live on.

This means women should be prepared to navigate the financial world on their own in their golden years.

George: So what are some meaningful life options?

Kerry: OK. That's the harsh reality for many women. But it's not all a desperate scenario of gloom and doom. Women are plainly increasing their share of both income and wealth in many sectors of our society. Many women today are in a stronger financial position than in previous generations. Increasingly, women are significant breadwinners.

Boomer women have worked and earned more than any previous generation, increasing their retirement savings as they go. Boomer women are earning their own Social Security benefits and will receive bigger Social Security checks, adjusted for inflation, than women in the past. Moreover, more of us will have our own pensions and retirement accounts than our mother's generation.

Women are starting their own businesses. They have savings and are, in many instances, better investors than their male counterparts. They have characteristics, in my opinion, that help them tally up better investment returns than men because they're not in it to outperform the market. They're in it for their long-term goals, so it is slow and steady with thoughtful decisions based on doing their research, and they're less likely to jump ship and sell if the market takes a dip. Studies from Vanguard and Fidelity also back me up on this better investor reality.

And many Boomer women can look forward to two or more inheritances. One may come from their husbands, who'll likely predecease them; women live roughly four years longer than men, on average. Another bequest could be the gift of parents or in-laws. Money or assets might even be passed along by siblings.

By some estimates, as much as two-thirds of all wealth in the U.S. will be controlled by women by the year 2030. And women tend to be philanthropists. They give back.

Change can be slow and inexorable, the way glaciers sliding to the sea used to be or how a sunflower grows from a seed to a mature plant. Change can also be fast and permanent like Krakatoa exploding or the moment Neil Armstrong first set foot on the Moon.

You can't think of change as being homogenous. The change model I prefer is the distinction between Continuous Change and Discontinuous Change. They aren't just opposites. There is usually a continuum of possibilities between them. Why is this especially important for people After 50? Because these types of changes— and the continuum between them—are different from our habit of only paying attention to the Continuous Change to which we are accustomed. Enter frequent but not regular Discontinuous Change. If you cannot see the difference, you will make the mistake of approaching them in identical ways and using identical tools. This, as you will see, can get people After 50 nowhere and cost both time and resources for no progress.

First I will talk about the two types of change from my perspective. Then we'll listen in on an interview I conducted with Steve Carnevale. He brings a strong business perspective to understanding change. He also brings a strong family perspective. Like a lot of us, he is living in both arenas as well as the After 50 arena simultaneously.

Continuous Change

Continuous Change isn't new. If you are about age 50, the kind of change with which you are most likely to be familiar is Continuous Change. Think cars. Standard transmission to automatic. Crank windows to push button. Think whitewall tires with tubes to all-weather tires without. Think education. Graduating from the fourth to the fifth to the sixth grades. Think work and career in a stable company and profession, moving gradually but continually up the ladder toward eventual retirement. Think dating to wedding to children and/or house to PTA and the kids' sports to empty nesters to retirement and golden years. Think wood stoves to electric to microwaves to convection; think brooms to upright and canister vacuums to built-in vacuum systems to robotic vacuums. At the time they were discontinuous because something stopped—cooking on a wood stove for instance. In hindsight we can see the longer, continuous trend continuing.

You get the point. Gradual, continuous change and improvement. It was clearly visible most of the time. Although it may have been advertised as revolutionary to earn your business, it wasn't really. And we don't always like it. In my current car you have to slide your finger across a bar to increase or decrease sound volume. I'd much rather have the old knobs back because I didn't have to take my eyes of traffic to use them as I do with the finger-sliding technology.

Discontinuous Change

Discontinuous Change isn't new either, but is increasingly a greater and greater percentage of the change we are facing. The advent of cell phones that were also cameras, texting devices, app machines, and financial information accessors led directly to the rapid decline of cell phones that were only phones, home/landline telephones, and branch banking. For the traditional telephone companies and the banks, this was definitely discontinuous change in how they did business, the jobs they needed to fill, the expectations of their customers, and the way we think of communication and banking. If you are older than age 50, you have likely experienced Discontinuous Change in the form of a divorce or a major illness or a sudden, large inheritance, although you may not have known the term or distinguished it from Continuous Change in making your plans and life decisions.

I think the distinction between Continuous and Discontinuous Change, plus being aware of the continuum between the two and all of those possibilities, is another key After 50 awareness we need to cultivate.

In fact, I think it's so important that I'm going to bring in another expert here before I go on with my own explanations. What follows is an interview with my colleague Steve Carnevale. He's a University of Michigan grad and the father of 18-year-old twin sons. He is an investor and a veteran of Silicon Valley and has served on many not-for-profit boards. We have been friends and colleagues for so long that no matter who is asking the questions, it becomes a lengthy and lively discourse. (For more about Steve, see www.PointCypressVentures.com.)

George: Let's begin by talking about what Discontinuous and Continuous Change means.

Steve: OK. So I think my general notion of it is that Continuous Change is incremental and Discontinuous Change is not incremental; it is a dramatic shift in thinking about something.

George: Give me an example of Continuous Change in the workplace and one in our personal lives.

Steve: Let's talk about it in the workplace. In the workplace, Continuous Change is what I would call the normal world where people are pretty comfortable with whatever environment they're in and they're trying to make it a little bit better and looking for pushing the edges of progress, in whatever that means. In Discontinuous Change, you're thinking about breaking your entire business model and pursuing a whole different strategy typically because you're in crisis, and so it's a much more radical thought. The business model is in many ways the equivalent of an individual's set of plans, habits, and expectations to lead a successful life.

George: Then let's take it down to the individual worker level.

Steve: I think the individual worker level in general is cast with execution and they're not pursuing Discontinuous Change. It isn't part of their daily lives at home or at work, generally, which can put them at a disadvantage when they get to retirement and their own, extended later lives. The worker and their jobs are usually aligned with productivity and Continuous Change. The Discontinuous Change that I have experienced is always created or recognized at an executive level where you have to dramatically change the way the business does things.

I think the human condition is by definition one of Continuous Change, and very few people set themselves up to easily look at or willingly think about Discontinuous Change because it's painful to reexamine everything—what is done, how it's done, whether or not it makes sense anymore, and what, if anything, should be done instead.

I was thinking the other day about the fact that, when we have children, it's hard to comprehend that this little child is going to be big someday.

I was looking at my sons just yesterday. It feels very natural now but I remember looking at them and not imagining them grown up when they were still 10. Now that they are tall, I realize that these processes happen slowly, incrementally enough that they're easy to digest.

So the process of life itself is one that evolves relatively slowly and relatively incrementally—Continuous Change—unless there is something that occurs that changes. That could be an earthquake, it could be that you're suddenly out of a job and now you have to move. It could be that your wife decides to divorce. We seldom invest in the future in such a way that it would prepare us for Discontinuous Change even if we see it coming and realize that we're going to need to prepare ourselves. We aren't attuned to the difference between the two kinds of change and I think we're going to need to be as the pace of change all around us increases and what we used to take for granted may no longer be reliable.

George: That's actually very interesting because I find myself now wondering if it's just that we are so good at adapting to Continuous Change that we neither discern the difference nor change our actions until we're really forced into a crisis mode. And even then we will want to stick to our tried-and-true ways.

Steve: I think we live in blissful denial in most aspects of our personal life and we also know that some of us as human beings are pretty good at Continuous Change and some people aren't very good at it.

George: How about businesses?

Steve: So let's go to the corporate level. How do businesses work with continuing Discontinuous Change? Well, again my experience has been that companies are just like people, only maybe worse. There's a momentum that goes on and the complexity of working with everybody; even if you know you need to change it is very hard because now it isn't just one person making the decision to change. You have to come up with a collective decision to change and even if you're the CEO it's very hard to harness that collective recognition that you need to change proactively as opposed to reactively, and so in a company situation we often don't change in a major way unless we're faced with a crisis. And this same thing can also happen in families where one person recognizes the need for change and has a difficult time getting other family members on board and thinking/ acting in a different way.

George: Let's talk about After 50. It seems to me that the issue isn't just acceleration and quantity of change. It's also that we have more Discontinuous Change. For instance, as much as retirement has been held as a gold standard, an increasing portion of the population is not going to be able to afford to or want to live that dream. They will live longer, have to work longer, and will need to be engaged and do things they think are worthwhile. This means Discontinuous Change for employers, employees, coworkers, ways of making money, career designs, health care, housing, product and service design, and transportation, just to name a few.

Steve: Well, before I answer that, I think you've raised an interesting question, which is even if you can afford to not face Discontinuous Change because you can temporarily buy your way out of it, there becomes an interesting question of whether that is really the right answer or not. Having plenty of money allows you to not change at all, but that doesn't mean that that's the right thing to do for you or your family.

George: Or the healthy thing to do.

Steve: Exactly. Because you might continue to propagate behaviors that are either bad for you or don't optimize the life that could be good for you. You don't change because you don't have to and that's part of the problem of not having a crisis when the change might actually create a better life for you. I think that that's a whole interesting dynamic in getting people to do it consciously and proactively rather than reactively, and therefore maybe not at all if they have enough money to react.

George: My wife and I decided to take the chance and move across the country to where we knew no one while we were still young enough to go back if we wanted to. We determined that if we could successfully build a life from scratch in our late 50s, nothing could happen to us in the future for which we didn't have the adaptive mind-set and skills.

Steve: So it seems like there are multiple things here. One is the recognition that Discontinuous Change is something that you need to actively think about and you're likely going to need to respond to. If you really want to maximize your life, and you have got a long life left After 50, you have to put yourself in the mind-set of challenging yourself on an ongoing basis.

George: So what are the biggest factors in resilience, then, from your standpoint?

Steve: I think some of them are believing that you can change. I think some of them are envisioning, having the skill set to being able to envision an alternate future. And I think that, just like in many other circumstances, we're better at doing that for other people than for ourselves. It is hard to see ourselves differently. And so you need enlightened external friends or change professionals who can be change agents, some external reference that helps you see that you have the capacity to do things that you didn't know existed or didn't know you had or could learn.

George: What am I not asking you about regarding Continuous and Discontinuous Change that I need to be asking you about?

Steve: Yes. Why do we care?

George: I care because as people approach 50 or leave 50 behind, most of us are pretty good at Continues Change—my car is wearing out; I can go and buy a new car; my kids are leaving; I am going to grieve but I am going to invest in them and help them move on.

As a grandparent I think it's my job to give my grandchildren discontinuous experiences. Sometimes with me and sometimes just arranged by me. They usually involve well-supervised opportunities, people they don't know, an opportunity to learn something brand new that stretches their sense of themselves. I try to arrange activities that are all within the safety of me knowing what will happen, dropping them off in the morning and picking them up in the afternoon, things like circus school, scuba diving, or theater camp.

My oldest granddaughter, almost 17, lived with my wife and me for a part of the summer doing an internship. It was her first experience of work, being responsible to people she doesn't know, living away from her immediate family, having her own wheels, and living—not visiting—on the other side of the country from her parents' home. This was intentional Discontinuous Change for her in full cooperation with her parents.

Steve: I care because I can see the difference in my future and my sons' future as a result of a combination of Continuous and Discontinuous Change. If we cannot always see in advance and be prepared, and by definition we cannot, then what are the skills, disciplines, and awarenesses we all must have to live high-quality lives in the future?

How about those of us over 50? Would we be wise to hand-pick and participate in Discontinuous Change experiences that would benefit us by increasing our adaptability and awareness? You bet we would. Can touring a foreign country, seeing it from the inside of a bus, surrounded by people like us, be an enlightening experience? Yes. But is it likely to be deeply discontinuous? It depends upon how separate we are from the experience. If we only get off the bus to see local dancers perform and then we get back on the bus, we're clearly quite separate from the experience. If we get off the bus and spend three to four weeks working in a local village school teaching English and live with a local family while doing so, we are having an immersion experience. Likely it will be a discontinuous one that surprises us by challenging our assumptions and giving us the gift of growing awareness and greater adaptability.

I am not suggesting that all of us over 50 should go live and work in a foreign village. I am suggesting, however, that 1) finding, 2) choosing, and 3) benefiting from discontinuous experiences is an individual responsibility that can be done near home and far away, too.

It seems to me that over 50 is exactly the time to make sure we are skilled at working with Continuous Change and Discontinuous Change because it is going to happen. Why wait until a Discontinuous Change—loss of spouse, illness, household move far away by people we are accustomed to depending on, termination of jobs and industry that we have taken for granted, winning the lottery and suddenly having to be a wise investor and consumer at a whole different level—has roared through our lives and left us in the situation of simultaneously developing the skills we need and solving/resolving what we are now facing?

EMILE AND FRANCINE

Emile and Francine, in their early 70s, came to me for personal consulting. Nothing was wrong. They were retired with enough money. They got along beautifully and were, in fact, the envy of their friends for their harmony together. In my book they were especially smart. Knowing they had no problem to solve didn't deter them. They knew something was going to come along that would be discontinuous in nature. "How could I help them?" they wanted to know. As we talked, we all realized they wanted support in 1) finding, 2) choosing, and 3) benefiting from early learning about something they would face in the future. When I asked them what they most feared, they both said being alone without the other one. As we explored the kinds of learning available to them, we realized that "being alone" wasn't the real issue at all. Being satisfied as an individual was the issue. It had been decades since they felt like individuals.

During all these years they had been "joined at the hip." To treat this as a problem and solve it would, in my opinion, have dishonored what they had been so proud of all these years. What non-problem-and-solution approach did we take? We decided they each wanted to face the discontinuous likelihood that they would survive the other one. Therefore, learning, not problem and solution, was the desired experience. We had found what they wanted. As for choosing, they took my recommendation that they take one day a week off from each other (they chose Thursdays) and actively explore and experience being an individual with their own interests and activities. We didn't dishonor their relationship. We added another dimension to their lives: greater independence and individuality. One got active in volunteering on Thursdays. The other went to work for a business start-up on Thursdays. They reported that their

Thursday evening dinner conversations were increasingly lively. And they were happy for each other. They had had the courage to experiment with a kind of learning that would give them the experience to deal with the Discontinuous Change of loss when the time came. They didn't expect it to be perfect, but whoever survived the other wouldn't have to begin to cope from scratch.

Like my granddaughter, Emile and Francine had a future that would involve both Continuous and Discontinuous Change. Being older wouldn't spare them that. Also like my granddaughter, they took the leap and benefited greatly from doing it wisely.

Before we finish, let's pursue some more specific information about change and how it can affect retirement planning, life planning, and our living our futures generally. I think most of us get Continuous Change. Here is a way to think about Disruptive Change.

Think about the new ways of driving: We are facing the advent of cars that drive themselves from auto manufacturers new to the marketplace. The impact on jobs that required drivers and vehicles could be enormous and very disruptive.

Think education. College graduation is no longer a guarantee either of short- or long-term employment. The shelf life of usable knowledge is much shorter. Lifelong learning and skills updating will be assumed. The concept of a four-year degree as a bundled, discrete step into maturity and a learning experience and then you are done is unravelling rapidly. Colleges are going to have to be competitive in new ways that will change their models. Universities and colleges are already increasingly being assessed in terms of graduates' employability and employment including compensation. Since most colleges and universities weren't designed to perform on this metric, an earthquake of change is happening. That's disruptive.

Think politics. We used to have two parties that were reasonably distinct from each other. There was campaigning and we knew that trusting our election process and institutions was a fundamental part of perpetuating democracy. Candidates disagreed but generally treated each other respectfully in public. Where are we now? Think back to the recent presidential campaign and election!

Think the use of all possible learning resources all the time. My friend Dick Bolles, 90, the internationally known author of the bestselling career book *What Color Is Your Parachute 2017*, told me in an interview how important paying attention and learning is to him at every age. "What I know about me is that anytime I see anything—I watch TV most nights with my wife and each night we watch a Western or a mystery or a foreign film—I'll see something in the pictures we're watching that makes me curious. So I never watch TV without my iPhone right at hand. The minute I get curious about something, I go straight to Wikipedia on my phone to find out more about it. If I see something about a historical period, I'll look it up to see if it's accurate or not. If I see an old-time actor or actress, I wonder what ever happened to him or her and I'll look to see what really did happen. So the thing that characterizes my life is endless curiosity. I'm not just sitting there watching movies. I am sitting there constantly learning."

Think work. Jobs and companies are no longer remotely permanent. Skills and expertise must be updated on a regular basis. Lifelong employment for all intents and purposes doesn't exist. Freelancing may possibly be as important to earning a living as jobs are. Work for pay may decreasingly be configured as a job. Robotics, software, and other technologies are replacing middle management and other bulwarks of the middle class. Disruptive.

Think marriage. Divorce is common and socially acceptable. In 1990, only one in 10 divorces involved people ages 50 and older. Now it's one in four. The over-50 divorce rate is even higher among those who remarried. The institution of marriage and its purposes are fundamentally changing for people After 50.

Think retirement planning. Think life planning. Think planning period. Interim, iterative, adjustable planning with a much shorter planning horizon is the emerging norm. Successful planning is now shorter term and success looks like the plan, and we ourselves adapt as required. Gone are the days when long-term retirement and life plan success is measured by flawless execution of a permanent plan.

Think about the distinction between retirement planning and life planning. It has almost entirely disappeared.

PUTTING CHANGE IN PERSPECTIVE WITH OUR NEW UNDERSTANDING

We've looked at change in detail, especially continuous and discontinuous. It's very important that you understand these concepts AND you pay attention to the continuum between them.

Many changes can be experienced as a hybrid of the two, measured in the amount of stability or discontinuity that's caused as a result of the change overall. A forest fire that destroys everything in its path for a month will be discontinuous to the homeowners who lost their houses with no notice as it swept across the countryside. Seen (perspective again) from the historic perspective over the centuries, that fire may be considered an example of Continuous Change.

Also, what's Continuous Change to you may be discontinuous to someone else. The company that employed you for years was recently sold, and massive layoffs are happening across the board. You were going to retire anyway in a few months, so you've accelerated your retirement date. The woman at the desk next to yours is 40 years old and a single mother with three kids. She didn't see this coming and hasn't done any job search since she was hired seven years ago. For her this will probably be highly Discontinuous Change.

It is crucial that people After 50 be able to manage their planning with their eyes on both continuous and discontinuous . . . and on everything in between. We often don't see Continuous Change because it isn't dramatic. We often don't see Discontinuous Change because it is so system-altering that it's upon us before we realize how this systemic change is going to affect important aspects of our lives and plans. Nevertheless, successful planning and successful adaptation requires a willingness to see and a skill adapting to both kinds of change and the continuum between them.

What is important for all of us to realize, as we plan and execute and adapt and then plan and act and adapt some more in incremental stages, is that Discontinuous Change in our lives must be managed differently from Continuous Change. Continuous Change often requires an updating of the plan accordingly.

Discontinuous Change usually requires major revision of the plan and how it is executed. Or it drives the need for a new plan altogether. Failing to distinguish between the two can put you behind the Eight Ball rapidly. Unfortunately, it's hard to catch up later if you weren't paying attention as you went along.

In my opinion, many vestiges of the Old Normal are still with us and will continue to be. The process of Continuous Change is so gradual that we won't notice. In many ways we prefer it because we can usually see it coming, somehow frame it as a problem to be solved or an opportunity to be resolved, come up with a solution, and move on to what's next. Working well with Discontinuous Change is a lot more work than that.

Also in my opinion, many vestiges of the Old Normal will continue to be blown away by Discontinuous Change that we don't see coming and therefore can't prepare for. It's going to be crucial for many of us After 50 to develop the capacity to see what's really going on around us and make important distinctions to be able to handle it well.

Reader Exercise

When was the last time you drove home or rode the subway and remembered everything you saw? When was the last time you arrived at home with no recollection of the streets or traffic lights or faces in the crowd? If we paid attention to everything all the time, we'd never have time for anything else. On the other hand, many of us have developed the ability to go through our daily lives without the need to think about things from tying our shoes to the route home. This means we're running the risk of not really seeing some important aspects of our lives. The following questions are intended to get us to take a closer look with conscious perspective. They are also intended to get us to name important information—current circumstances and future expectations—because unless we name it, we can't work with it now or going forward. And you will need to do that in order to gain the maximum return from this book.

1. What does normal look like in your life at your current age?
2. What kinds of Continuous Change are happening in your life now?

3. What kinds of Discontinuous Change are happening in your life now?
4. What kinds of change are possible in your life over the next 25 years?
5. Which changes will be chosen by you and which will happen without your permission?

•••

The most common form of retirement and life planning usually says: Find your bliss/purpose and pursue it with gusto. The underlying logic for this path is:

1. You only have one bliss or purpose and you just haven't found it yet. That is a significant failure or omission on your part so far.
2. This "bliss" is waiting there for you with open arms. All you have to do is name it and make it your life's purpose. With enough passion, everything else will pretty much fall into place.
3. Like the American Work Dream ("Just work hard and you will get there, kid, even if you have to pull yourself up by your bootstraps"), there isn't much room in this approach for what it will take, if there will be any demand for it, or if others have gotten there before you and will be appalled at the notion of sharing.
4. It's a pretty linear and solitary thing: Figure it out, go after it, and get there. There isn't much provision here for anything morphing, being discontinuously changed, or simply disappearing along the way.
5. There is absolutely no provision for the possibility that the experience will change you along the way and you might then want to choose and pursue an alternative or aligned bliss or purpose.

I am perfectly willing to subscribe to the notion that you have life purposes that you brought with you or created.

I am equally willing to subscribe to the notion that bliss or joy is connected to and even a by-product of you exploring your purposes. No one wants to do something he/she doesn't like at all, much less for the rest of his/her life.

What I am NOT willing to subscribe to is the seductive, even tantalizing, notion that great retirement and life planning begins by imagining your future and working backward to your present based on imagining your bliss. It's all too easy to fall in romantic love with the future you imagine and never do an adequate job of assessing where you are. It's essential that we do the more difficult but ultimately far more productive and grounded work of assessing where we are before we leap into our imaginations and sally forth into our futures.

There is another very strong reason to work from the present forward to the future. Take a close look After 50 at who our heroes used to be: cowboys, visionary but often solitary pioneers, soldiers, courageous individuals who struggled against great odds as workers for social change like civil rights and union representation, fictional/unique characters like Superman and Batwoman, men and women who have crossed known boundaries to travel into and walk in space, inventors who built (digital or not) products that changed our lives from airplanes to software, great but tragic figures who gave their lives for us and our country like John F. Kennedy and Sharon Christa McAuliffe and Judith A. Resnik and Martin Luther King, and men and women of enduring accomplishment who we could hold up as worthy models indefinitely.

What do many of these people have in common?

1. They had a dream they pursued, often alone until they built a network of engaged others.
2. They set out to right wrongs or create something new we had not previously imagined.
3. They seized the initiative and often could control the mini-environment in which they were working as long as disaster didn't happen.

4. They lived in a time when (for good or bad) significant social/professional class tiers or hierarchy and academic/professional/financial qualifications were important for credibility and to get attention.
5. They lived in a time when societies were comparatively low tech: telephones, television, and newspapers. Innovations were, for the most part, extensions of current technologies (i.e., Maxwell Smart's shoe phone and the Batmobile).

What's different now and what does it mean for retirement and life planning?

1. The body of information is vast and growing exponentially. No matter how smart or educated we are, no one can know it all (or even close) anymore. Information is assaulting us 24-7.
2. We need to make instant decisions about where to invest our attention and energy. We can't absorb it all as we become increasingly saturated.
3. We are no longer in a fixed or slow-moving, manufacturing-oriented economy. Instead we're in a fast-paced, rapidly changing, highly networked service economy that depends upon new and evolving technologies to proceed, maneuver, and hold it all together.
4. Our futures and—like it or not—the quality of our lives is growing increasingly dependent upon our active memberships in a range of networks to have access to the information, the right kinds of relationships, and to increase the likelihood of getting the outcomes we want. We're going to become more, not less, interdependent with people we know well and those we don't. We're going to have to understand how to operate well under those circumstances or risk losing out and being marginalized at best. This goes directly to the heart of successful life and retirement planning.

Many of us (including myself) After 50 complain from time to time that our grandchildren like to text us at most four- to six-word messages and can pay far more attention to their tablet devices than they do to us.

If you are 55 or 65 or 75 and have a strong desire for financial capacity, meaningful engagement, belonging, and stimulation, how likely is it that you can accomplish them without ramping ourselves up to participate along with the rest of the world in leveraging the networks and technologies on which life is increasingly running? I argue that it is unlikely or even impossible for us to limit ourselves to dated approaches and preferences, no matter how comfortable they are, if we expect to get and accomplish what we want in the years and decades remaining in our lives.

This has a huge impact on what smart retirement and life planning looks like and how we must go about it.

What we now know with certainty:

- There are a lot of us facing this need for retirement and life planning. We aren't alone. We also aren't identical. One shape of life or retirement planning or execution won't fit everyone by a long shot.
- There is a revolution happening in the shape of retirement. We're going to have to craft our own best-fit version for ourselves.
- There is a revolution happening in both retirement planning and life planning. We're going to have to be much better at incremental, shorter-term planning and be ready to adapt both the plan and ourselves as necessary. The plan will have to be a living, breathing part of us rather than something we put on paper and store in a drawer.
- Regardless of our previous background and experience, we're going to have to think and act more like the strategic and tactical CEO of our lives rather than as an employee expecting the larger strategies to be handed to us for tactical execution.

RECAP OF WHAT WE'VE COVERED SO FAR

Let's go a step further and have a short recap of where we've been in this book so far. This is essential to avoid falling into the trap of thinking, "Oh! That was interesting," and then leaping directly back into our accustomed, less-informed ways of thinking, planning, and acting.

According to the U.S. Census Bureau and AARP, we are a population of 108.7 million people age 50 plus. Of this total, 53.5 million are women and 55.2 million are men.

We are often lumped under labels like Baby Boomer and Traditionalist—based on birth year—as if we were vastly more alike than we are different.

Retirement used to be universally understood as a discrete life stage when you didn't work anymore and were entering into golden years of leisure.

Retirement now—although we may leave our full-time, recent employment—doesn't necessarily suggest not working. All it means is that we're facing a large menu of possibilities, some of which we'll have to create and some of which will be presented to us. The fact that we still use the word *retirement*, as outdated as it is, won't change until there is a newer and more accurate descriptor that comes along. Until then we're stuck with retirement.

The truth is that, while we have many similarities and needs in common, in practice there could be almost as many forms of "retirement" in practice as there are numbers of us. One shape will not fit all.

Our After 50 lives are going to be different from our parents' and grandparents' because the world is different and so are we. Having survived the Great Depression and WWII, they, understandably, craved lives of stability with clear rules, roles, and as little Discontinuous Change as possible. How realistic is that for us today in today's world?

The real work before us After 50 is to stop thinking of retirement as a stage of life and begin to understand that what we are really doing is planning for multiple, overlapping components of our lives. For some people, work will be a part of it for a long time, if not indefinitely. For some of us—with the financial capacity—it will mean leaving work behind.

To succeed at planning, executing, plan revision, adapting, and executing some more, holding multiple perspectives will be crucial. We will also need to identify, comprehend, and alter—as necessary—the major life models we have used to think, make decisions, and act. This will, of course, require challenging our own assumptions periodically.

We will need to be able to understand, identify, and work with all the forms of change that will come into our futures. This will require paying attention. For some of us this could be uncomfortable. For many of us it could be awkward at first just as every new kind of work is in the beginning.

The After 50 years aren't just another set of decades. They contain two huge gifts—gifts that we'll have to accept and nurture to realize their potential.

1. We can continue to grow, change, and evolve, individually and collectively.
2. We can understand and take advantage of the years After 50 as years that are valuable and exciting in their own right AND that serve as the runway for the quality of life in our later years. A great 12-year-old doesn't start at age 11. A great 91-year-old doesn't start at age 90.

However old you are now, your future deserves a well-informed plan adaptable you. It's never too late to begin. It's never too late to update.

This leads to what you need to explore in crafting your retirement and your life plan. What are essential questions you need to ask and answers you need to find for your short-term, medium-range, and long-term future?

chapter 4

Getting Real: Imagine Your Future and Start Planning

The place to begin, as I often say, is where we are. It's fun to imagine the future, and we need to do that, but that imagining frequently fails to become actionable unless we start with where we are. It's too easy to get lost in the joys of possibilities and frequently too painful to look in the mirror and acknowledge where we are. Where are we?

Generally, we're over 50 and have some growing level of awareness that many of us—not all but many—could have a longer future in front of us than our grandparents did. At 50, a substantial number of us could potentially live, need to pay for, and want to find engagement and meaning for another 30 to 50 years. As you can see, it's not just about money and financial planning. It's about interests, engagement, belonging, and quality of life for potentially a long time. Those additional 50 years used to be an entire lifetime.

Imagine you are standing onstage, about to describe a rhinoceros to your very diverse audience. You can't see their faces because of the stage lights. You are glad they are out there because you are deeply interested in their welfare. They all came voluntarily and need to hear your information. Knowing about rhinos is already essential to their futures, although many don't know that yet. Some audience members are extremely rhino-informed and, far across the bell curve, some have never heard of a rhino before. The majority, in the middle, know rhinos exist and maybe even saw one once but didn't find it interesting or important enough to pay closer attention. Where do you start? With the horn end, the tail end, the dimensions, their environment, or the evolutionary history? How much detail should you include?

FINANCIAL LITERACY

The rhino dilemma is what I am facing as we begin to talk here about financial literacy, one of the most important sets of knowledge we need to anticipate and include as we plan for our retirements and extended lives. Unless financial literacy is our profession and passion, we're all going to need different types of information and financial advisors for different purposes at different times in our lives. We all need to be financially literate enough to understand where we are and what we face in getting to where we need to be, even with professional support.

I am going to provide some core financial literacy information here. Only you know how financially literate you are right now. Only you will be in the position of proactively going after additional financial knowledge that builds upon what I will include here.

I strongly encourage you to invest time and effort in yourself and in your future by continuing the development of your financial literacy. If you are part of a couple, both of you should make the investment. You can explore financial literacy online. You can take consumer classes provided by your community or either the not-for-profit organizations or the for-profit businesses that offer financial education. You can explore in-person and online courses provided by colleges and universities. You can explore state and federal consumer education and financial literacy websites for additional information. Financial literacy isn't a static or unchanging body of knowledge. Like most knowledge, it changes subtly or dramatically over time. Your financial literacy, once acquired, must be refreshed and updated periodically.

Beware of offers of "free" anything: education, services, materials, consulting time, books, online access, or software. Think "two free nights at our resort for just sitting in our timeshare presentation for 90 minutes." "Free" usually means—although the content of what you are given may be fine—that you have signed up for not only a sales pitch but one that is carefully crafted, rehearsed, and staged. I am not saying don't sign up. I am saying do expect to be "sold" something at some point, and keep your wits about you always. Remember especially your ability to say "No!" and your strength to simply leave if sales pressure is applied. This selling can be obvious or very subtle. Pay close attention whenever you get involved in anything offered for "free"!

Financial literacy is generally understood to be the ability to manage personal finance matters in an efficient and informed manner. It includes the knowledge of making appropriate decisions about personal finance such as investing, insurance, real estate, paying for college, budgeting, retirement, and tax planning.

The lack of financial literacy can be what gets us into trouble. According to The President's Advisory Council on Financial Literacy, about the financial crisis of 2008:

> *"Far too many Americans signed loan agreements they did not understand. Sadly, far too many Americans do not have the basic financial skills necessary to develop and maintain a budget, to understand credit, to understand investment vehicles, or to take advantage of our banking system. It is essential to provide basic financial education that allows people to better navigate an economic crisis such as this one. Financial illiteracy is not an issue unique to any one population. It affects everyone—men and women, young and old, across all racial and socio-economic lines. No longer can we stand by and ignore this problem. The economic future of the United States depends on it."* For more information go to http://jumpstart.org/assets/files/PACFL_ANNUAL_REPORT_1-16-09.pdf.

I am not assuming here that you are or are not financially literate.

I am, however, making four assumptions that I'd like you to understand:

1. We can all benefit from regular financial literacy refreshers. Regardless of chronological age, if you are 24 or 75, financial literacy is increasingly an essential component of knowing where we are and how we can get to where we want to be. It requires knowledge. It also requires discipline. Financial literacy may mean one thing to someone who, at 24, is in her first paid job and is either working toward or has just finished her college degree. She won't have lots of assets or, perhaps, income but she must be literate and attentive to what she does have and manage it well so that this becomes a lifelong habit. Her financial advisor may be a bookkeeper or CPA who can teach her the methods and tools of smart budgeting. It may mean something different to someone who is 55 and has just found a job after being involuntarily unemployed for 18 months. He may have depleted some or most of his assets. His spouse may be working. They need to build financially again. They must work together to practice financial literacy to get where they want to go. A financial advisor for them may be a specialist in investments that build more rapidly with limited risks than other options. A 75-year-old recent widow may have an entirely different perspective on financial literacy. Perhaps she was a professional who maintained a career and a family. Perhaps she became and remained financially literate throughout. Perhaps she left the financial arrangements to her husband and, suddenly, must become financially literate in a big and regrettable hurry now. She may need two advisors: an investment professional and a tax professional. There is no rule that says she can only have one.

2. Many of us have fallen and continue to fall into the habit of outsourcing responsibility for our ultimate financial well-being and security. We outsource our retirement savings to our employers and the investment companies that run their programs including savings matching. We outsource our personal savings and other assets to bankers and financial advisors. We outsource the durability and duration of our income streams (which we call jobs) to the leadership of the companies we work for. I am

not suggesting we shouldn't do these things. I am suggesting it's a terrible idea to do these things and then forget about them, failing to regularly understand what is really happening with them, for extended periods of time.

3. It's likely when you talk about your assets that you limit your conversation to those assets convertible to cash quickly or slowly. You have other assets that should be included in your inventory AND that should be managed accordingly over time.

4. My readers are a very diverse group of people. Some of you are highly and actively financially literate. Regardless of age, many of you have left the understanding and management of your daily finances to someone else: a spouse, a CPA, an advisor, or serendipity. In my judgment, the coming years will mandate that each and every one of us without exception be highly financially literate and informed/engaged in all the daily and periodic financial reviews and decisions necessary to assure our good financial health. Financial literacy not only includes understanding your inventory, it also includes understanding—and ease of use with—at least one form of personal financial management software such as Quicken, Moneydance, Buxfer, Banktree, or Moneyline. Do your research. Scan the Internet for comparisons and evaluations that can point the way to the best one for you.

Note: I am not a financial advisor or expert. What I have written here is based on my own experience, including as a personal consultant to hundreds of clients over many years. The following primer is a great place to start. However, you will need to substantially add to it to have real financial literacy.

Developing financial literacy is an essential requirement for real adulthood.

Where would you rank your financial literacy on a scale of 0 (low; clueless) to 5 (exposed but not knowledgeable) to 10 (high; fully informed and up to date)?

Some of this may seem basic to you and if it is, you can skip ahead. For others, this may be the first time you have looked at this important information and linked it directly to your retirement and your entire future.

Let's begin.

1. From the time we are approaching independence in work and living arrangements, each of us needs to take more responsibility for our current and future financial health than anyone else takes. In fact, it's a very good idea, whenever possible, to learn through participation in financial review discussions inside our families before we leave the nest.

2. Assets are commonly understood to be what we own. The asset's net value to us is the difference between its market value and any outstanding debt (e.g., mortgage, credit card, personal loan, homeowner's line of credit) that was incurred in purchasing the asset.

3. Debts are commonly understood to be what we owe that has a remaining/outstanding balance.

4. If you are not familiar with balance sheets (statements of assets and liabilities), it's a very good idea to obtain a blank balance sheet (available online and at office supply stores) and fill it out for yourself/your family to see where you are in terms of assets and liabilities. Even if you are familiar with balance sheets, if you haven't done one on yourself or your family in some time, it's a very good idea.

5. Net income is generally understood to be the amount of pay or retirement benefits you bring home (in a check or direct deposit to your checking account) after taxes and withholdings are made. Take a close look at your pay slip to see how much of your gross/total income goes where before filing it away.

6. Expenses are generally understood to be what you spend your net income or retirement benefits on between paydays.

7. Budgets are projections of income and expense for a given, future period of time. They are used to track what you intended so that you can compare your budget to what happened.

8. Financial security for retirement used to be based on what financial advisors called the three-legged stool: Social Security, pension benefits, and personal savings. Pensions, of course, were "guaranteed" for life (after retirement) and inviolable. I think, where pensions still exist, this guarantee is no longer the case and we will be seeing many changes to pension payouts in coming years.

9. Financial security for retirement changed—and so did the three-legged stool—where expensive pension packages have been eliminated and employees began to be required to participate in retirement-specific savings programs (e.g., 401K) with and without employer-matching funding. Personal savings and Social Security continued to support the retirement funding stool.

10. Today I think we are clearly moving to a four-legged financial security stool:

   a. Retirement-specific savings programs, with or without employers' participation.

   b. Personal savings and equities (including assets such as home equity, securities, personal valuables such as art, and salable businesses).

   c. Social Security. The future of Social Security continues to be uncertain in the face of ongoing debates about entitlements.

   d. Extended work-related income streams from jobs, freelancing, or entrepreneurial efforts, or other sources that begin prior to retirement or are begun concurrent with or sometime after retirement. Why is the inclusion of D as a stool leg so important and even revolutionary? Because, first, it confirms what we have all been observing: that "retirement" and no longer working for money are no longer simultaneous. Second, it immediately calls into prominence the reality that many people—whether they do it primarily for money or engagement or health-care benefits or some mix of these—will work for much longer than traditional ideas of retirement allowed. People will need to be doing thoughtful and intensive career/employment planning in their 50s, 60s, and 70s at the very time in life when their parents (and they themselves until recently) expected to stop working forever.

11. Well prior to "retirement"—and as part of financial literacy and financial planning—you will need to know about and use regularly and wisely six key financial health strategies:

a. Make more money. Take a look at your own life today. What are ways in which you could increase your income? What should you do with the additional income?

b. Spend less money. Take a look at your own life today. What are ways in which you could reduce your expenses? What should you do with the monies saved by spending less?

c. Increase your return on your investments (ROI). Take a look at your own life today. What are the ways in which you could—without assuming unreasonable risk—increase the return on each of your investments including savings? What should you do with the additional monies you would receive? One of the most important—and automatically beneficial—ways to increase your ROI is to participate fully and consistently in retirement savings programs that involve employer-matching funding.

d. Budget well and stick to it. Take a look at your own life today. How well planned are your expenditures, large and small? How realistic is your budget? How closely do you stick to your budget? What should you do with the monies saved by smarter budgeting and expenditures?

e. Pay yourself first. Don't save from what's left. Save first and use the remainder for your ongoing budget and expenses.

f. Make financial projections. Look out into your retirement financial future. Advisors and journalists will offer easy rules of thumb. For instance, you will need 70 percent of your working income to be able to retire. For example, you will need at least $1,000,000 to increase the likelihood that you won't outlive your money. The fact may be that some of these generalizations may work for you. Or not. Most of these rules of thumb are for the "average" retiree. You are sitting on a bell curve along with all the other retirees. Where are you on the bell curve? Are you exactly average? I'm not saying you should ignore all the rules of thumb offered to you. I am saying the smartest approach is to sit down and budget/financially plan a representative year based on what you expect YOUR own expenses to be (and not bell curve averages) and multiply that times the number of years you will spend that much money. Then go back to the four-legged stool. Compute your future income. The difference will be your shortfall or your bonus.

Financial literacy should be part of all our futures. What I have provided to you here is intended to be stimulating and a platform from which to conduct the forms of financial learning and financial exploration that are right for you now and in the future.

• • •

In addition to giving you the strategies, I interviewed colleagues who are various types of financial advisors to get tips for you. Here they are:

1. Make savings an early habit. Save well and save often.
2. If your employer offers matching funds for your retirement savings contribution, take the maximum possible advantage of the program throughout your employment.
3. Don't be excessively swayed by rules of thumb such as, "You will need 70 percent of your working income during your retirement years." Or, "Everyone will need at least $1.5 million in retirement savings, given inflation and other adjustments." These numbers and rules of thumb are all based on many people on a bell curve with a weighted average. You probably don't sit at the middle of the bell curve. And you may not be average. The much better idea, while you are hearing the rules of thumb, is to take a long look at budgeting for your future and use rules of thumb to inform that, not the other way around.
4. Whether you have a little money or a lot, use a professional advisor regularly and wisely.

5. Don't assume that because someone works for a bank or other financial institution that he/she is qualified to advise you.
6. Spend less than you earn every year.
7. When looking seriously at retirement, don't assume it means you will never work again. That increasingly is not the case.
8. Hold the longer-term view. Expect to remain active and vigilant about finances so you don't accidentally outlive your money.
9. Both spouses in every couple's situation should be fully familiar with financial details and responsible for making all important financial decisions.

Remember, about financial literacy, that none of us will "graduate" and arrive at a place where we know it all in perpetuity. The fact is that like all other forms of expertise, it has a shelf life and requires regular renewal. How do I get there from here? One of the ways is financial literacy regularly supplemented by the support of well-chosen professionals.

TAKING INVENTORY OF OUR ASSETS

Now that you "get" financial literacy, I'd like to continue by taking an inventory of our current lives. The place to begin, as I said earlier, is where we are. It's fun to imagine the future, and we need to do that, but that imagining frequently fails to become actionable unless we start with where we are. How clear are you about where you really are?

This is going to be a different kind of asset inventory from the ones you may have made in the past. We're not just going to look at the kinds of assets to which we are accustomed. Limiting our asset review to the familiar tends to limit our thinking and confine us to the erroneous notion that if we just have enough money everything else will be okay. If we just have enough money, we will be protected and insulated from change that might affect other people, right? If we have enough money, we can simply figure it all out—health, community, activities, what is meaningful, friendships, ideal location, interests, professional connections, retirement, spouses and partners, volunteering, extended full- or part-time careers, grandchildren, and other key players—on the spur of the moment when the time comes, right? Unlikely!

In the future we will all have to monitor regularly the presence, absence, sufficiency, insufficiency, and trending of assets we're going to need.

After reading the following information thoroughly, I am asking you to conduct a thoughtful and thorough analysis of the condition of your assets, the assets upon which the quality of your future will depend. Once again, if you are married or have a partner, you should both do this together or at least share the information in detail.

For purposes of retirement and life planning, I am breaking assets into four categories:

1. Cash and Assets That Can Readily Be Converted to Cash
2. Other Assets
3. Current Skills (Yes, these are assets!)
4. Current Knowledge (Yes, this is an asset, too!)

You will note that I have listed both skills and knowledge. It's not uncommon for us to think if we have the skills that will be sufficient. It's also not uncommon for us to think we have the knowledge and that's sufficient.

In truth, it takes both—and our ability to quickly use them—because having the skill without the knowledge means we can mechanically act but fail to grasp any of the strategic importance or implications of what we are doing and why. Conversely, having the knowledge without the skill means we can understand but not act effectively in our own or others' best interest.

Take a laptop, tablet, or pencil and paper. Begin a written list of your assets and their estimated market value. For those assets with debt attached, be sure to include both the loan balance and the payment terms in the appropriate space. If you would like to make reminder notes to yourself of some kind, you can enter those in the Notes to Self column. See Figure 4-1.

Figure 4-1. Sample Asset List.

Asset (What Is It?)	Debt and Payment Terms (How Much Is Owed and When?)	Notes to Self (Anything You Need to Remind Yourself Of)

ASSETS

Cash and Other Assets That Can Readily Be Converted to Cash

Cash and cash balances in institutions. Investments. Real estate (ease of conversion to cash will vary with the asset and the market). Objects of monetary value you have in your home or office (ease of conversion to cash will vary with the asset and the market). Remember that any of these may have debt attached.

Terri and Alan, both in their late 40s, work full-time. He works in publishing. She is a nurse. They have two daughters, ages 12 and 16. They own their home. The net value of this asset is the difference between the market value of the house and the mortgage balance. They both have 401(K)s through their work. The total of the two 401(K)s is $120,000. They have $20,000 invested in stocks to help pay for the girls' college educations when the time comes. They have no other savings to speak of and few other assets of value. Or so they think.

Investments, Securities, Real Estate, and Other Assets That Cannot Readily Be Converted to Cash

It's important to be real and relatively unemotional about assets and their real value. Real estate, art, and other objects of monetary value may or may not be readily convertible to cash. If you are in doubt, consult a professional who specializes in that type of asset.

The equity Terri and Alan have in their house is about $100,000. The market value of the house is $325,000. Their mortgage balance is $225,000. The home is not readily convertible to cash. Even if they wanted/needed to sell it, it could take a while. There could be significant tax consequences to the sale. Their $120,000 in 401(K)s could be liquidated but the tax consequences could be huge. The $20,000 invested for the girls' college educations is in theory readily convertible to cash. But then they would have zero saved for the girls and, with a 16-year-old, the need is not that far away.

"Strong" Relationships

Relationships, especially in today's world when a single person cannot possibly capture or know all that needs to be known and must rely on others for information and expertise, are very important. Why are they assets? Because they have and bring value. Without them, our lives are impoverished.

Foremost among these relationships are people to whom we are strongly connected. Not only do we have strong relationship, we also have networks of strong relationships because many of these people know each other. This usually means that we have many values in common, probably have a fair amount of history together or can act as if we do, have high levels of trust, know many of the same people, often can finish each other's sentences, and can be absolutely counted to be there when needed. We can often start conversations with our strong connections as if we had just seen them two days ago when we have not talked for some time. The benefits of strong relationships lie in their efficiency (so little needs to be explained) and their reliability. Your sister can take one look at you and know what to do. Your neighbor can take your kids at a moment's notice without alarming anyone, especially the kids. Your business partner can see where you are going off the rails (again) and get you back on track, sometimes before you know there is a problem. You don't need to see them every day or live near them. The test is this: If after a period of disconnection, can you pick things up as if you had just seen each other last week?

There is no best number of strong relationships. The number of strong relationships needed may vary up and down across our lives. They must be nurtured and cannot be taken for granted for long. Sometimes strong relationships become weak ones simply because circumstances change and their usefulness is diminished. It's OK. Strong relationships are wonderful but don't have to be forever or lifelong to be valid.

Ginny and Bob were both 51 years old. They had an active social life, mostly based around their kids' sports and school activities. Their closest friends were people they had known since the kids began their early educations together. After the kids graduated and went away, Bob and Ginny noticed that without the glue and the propinquity of athletic events, the old connections began to slowly but surely fade away. They did not anticipate Ginny receiving the promotion she had been putting off for a long time. It involved a distant household move. Bob had his own small business and worked from home, so he was easily portable. Their expectations did not anticipate leaving the core of their relationship networks behind. Turnover, departures, and arrivals in core networks are to be expected. What do you imagine Bob and Ginny needed to do to restore their core networks?

John, 66, and his brother had been tightly connected since boyhood. They still lived around the corner from each other and their kids went to school together. Although they fought regularly, to everyone's surprise they remained best friends, nearly to the exclusion of anyone else. One night John's brother was killed in an auto accident. Except for his wife, John felt alone. He had been loving but not thoughtful enough about having "enough" strong relationships—a strong network—in his life.

Your Professional Identity, Connections, and Reputation

Regardless of your work or levels of income or education, if you are skilled at what you do—brain surgeon, carpenter, homemaker, airline pilot, baker, mechanic, publisher, or professional magician—you have a professional identity and a reputation. Begin to think of it as an asset, one that requires care and attention.

Mark, 47, and Gary, 55, had been a couple for many years. Mark flew for a major airline and was away from home several days per month. Gary worked for a major bank and was home every night. He was appreciated and promoted at the bank for his ability to cultivate new business and customer loyalty. When his bank merged with another, there was a significant round of layoffs and Gary lost his employment. The couple didn't see it coming, of course, but they weren't very surprised either, given the volatility of employment in our economy. They needed to sit down and take a much closer look not just at their finances but also their reemployability in the current work marketplace. They hadn't done this in a long time. Gary immediately began to take a closer look at what he was good at, the size and status of his professional network, how much of his expertise was current and how much might be outdated, and where in the world of work for pay there could be opportunities. He didn't limit himself to thinking only about jobs. He also considered freelancing, entrepreneurial work, and project-based work. Fortunately, he had paid attention to and nurtured his professional identity, reputation, and connections all along. They were assets. And he continued to stay actively connected to his networks of relationships. If you were in this situation, where would you have started and what is the outcome you would have eventually wanted?

"Weak" Relationships

We have already talked about "Strong Relationships." Of equal importance and value are "Weak Relationships." These relationships are not inferior to strong relationships but are different. These are people to whom we are loosely or weakly connected. Unlike strong relationships, these are people with whom we don't have a lot of history. We may not have identical values or share lots of interests. These aren't people you would immediately go to in an emergency. Often they are friends of our friends, colleagues of our colleagues, people we know slightly because our paths cross periodically. We can't finish each other's sentences. They usually don't know all the people we know. Yet we need them in our lives because they know people and are a source of information/possibilities that we don't even know about. Brand-new ideas, connections, and possibilities are MUCH more likely to come from weak relationships than from strong ones. They are great for challenging our thinking, opening our eyes to alternatives, and opening doors we did not know were there. Weak relationships also serve as the pool of candidates for new strong relationships.

Lisa, 52, and Don, 66, met when they worked for the same company several years ago. Lisa, who had always been overweight, was considering having surgery. Neither Don nor Lisa knew much about it nor did their friends. It happened that their neighbor's sister was a nurse and she was coming for a visit. She had not only observed the surgery, she had had it herself, realizing how common obesity is in nursing and knowing she had an advanced case. Their neighbor arranged for a morning coffee at her house that included Lisa, Don, their neighbor, and her sister. This connection through a connection opened doors to all kinds of possibilities and knowledge they hadn't known about.

Esther, 64, and Linda, 57, were a relatively new couple. Both had had long-term partners who died. As a recent couple, they had lots of sorting to do. Which relationships did they each want to keep? Which would fade away? Where did they want to live? What about work? Esther was ready to retire but Linda, who was a psychiatric nurse, was not. She never wanted to retire, although she did want to get more into hospital administration and give up direct patient care. They were both ready for a new start. Both wanted to live somewhere warm after many years in Buffalo. Smart women, they went to their friends to ask, "Who do you know who has recently moved to Arizona? Who do you know who is active in a national hospital professional organization? Who do you know who is starting a new, long-term and committed relationship at this point in their lives? Would you introduce us to these people and set it up so we can have a conversation with them and ask questions about their experiences?" Linda and Esther were seeking weak connections through the support and contacts of their strong connections. As it turned out, their strong connections could open all the doors they needed. Esther and Linda were then able to tap into these new, weak connections to obtain information that would not have been directly available through their strong connections.

"How did you arrive at your decision to move? What did you find out the hard way that you wish you had known in advance? If you had it to do all over again, what would you do and why? How are you defining retirement for yourself? What's it like when one partner is retired and one partner works? What has worked beautifully? What didn't?"

Professional Advisors You Can Rely On

Regardless of our age, educational level, profession, financial status, or life plan, we're all going to need professional advice from time to time. We can't individually know it all. With the help of professional advisors, we can remain proactive and on target when things are going according to plan. We are also going to need them—often in a hurry—when, as inevitably will happen, we get surprised and need to adapt.

These professional advisors can be tied to our physical and emotional health (doctors and therapists), our relationships (counselors), our financial health (financial advisors), careers (career experts), and retirement and life planning (personal consultants).

When considering professional advisors, it's crucial to remember that you may need more than one—based on specialty—and that someone who is a great advisor at one point in your life may not be the right person at another point.

Here is a health-care example:

Asa, 74, suddenly had kidney stone pain for the first time in his life. Fortunately, he had a health-care professional advisor, his personal physician, who quickly saw Asa in his office. His doctor immediately opened the door for Asa to see a great urologist. If Asa hadn't had his own health-care professional in place already, he would have had a much harder time and it would have taken much longer to get him to treatment.

Financial Advisors

In my opinion, every adult should, regardless of age, have a financial advisor who is the right person with the right knowledge for you at that moment. Who and what you need will not remain a constant. This advisory service doesn't have to be expensive or long term. Simply reaching out and having a financial conversation with a professional can be a big step forward whether that professional is a bookkeeper, CPA, stock and bond specialist, tax specialist, real estate professional, or someone else with the right set of experience and expertise for you at that time. It's very, very good practice as you go along to seek the advice of professionals periodically. Why?

1. It forces you to do your homework and be prepared with the most beneficial-to-you questions.
2. It grows your network of weak relationships.
3. It reminds you that doing things alone is not always the best approach.
4. It builds the skills required to calmly and wisely seek advice and choose the pieces of advice that are the best for you.
5. It stimulates your thinking by bringing up new information and helping you to see that you don't know what you don't know.

Financial Advisor Selection

The best way to find a great financial advisor is to ask members of your strong and weak relationship networks who they have successfully used and had a good experience with. You will need to be careful that what you need is in the same ballpark as what they needed and/or that their recommended person is a match for your needs.

A checklist of criteria for selection of the best financial advisor for your current needs:

- Does he/she walk the talk? How well does he/she practice the same financial advice in his/her own life? What is the track record of success? Whether the advisor is a bookkeeper teaching you about personal accounting software or a big-time investment professional advising you on the acquisition of real estate or securities, don't be afraid to ask direct questions about the advisor's own life and evidence of successfully walking the talk.

- Does the cost—large or small—of the prospective advisor's services feel like a good-value, appropriate investment in yourself and your future? Failure to invest wisely in yourself periodically can have long-standing consequences.
- Does this person have the professional credentials or certifications that establish him/her as a thought leader who is well recognized and respected by his/her colleagues?
- Does this person have a history of success in working with clients? Has he/she provided you with current client contact information so that you can ask about their experience?
- Does this person have a sub-agenda, like selling you investments on which he/she gets a commission? Remembering that all professionals deserve to be paid, it's important to make sure there is a complete match between what you need and what is provided.
- Does the pure interpersonal chemistry work? How well do you connect with this person? How honest can you be? How well does this person "get" you? How available are you to do your own work supported by this person?

Lisa is 24. She has graduated from college—with student debt—and is living and working at her first job in Chicago. She shares an apartment with another young woman, depends upon public transportation, and is careful with her money. She knows she is earning enough to support herself as long as she is careful. Having watched her parents fail to save, she is aware of the importance of saving. What woke her up at night was feeling as if she didn't have a close enough handle on her daily cash position and her spending patterns. Lisa decided she needed to learn to use a good home bookkeeping software package. She called that bookkeeper at her parents' business to get a software recommendation, priced it out, chose a software store that offered both online and in-store software training, and began what she hoped would be the lifelong habit of carefully managing her assets.

Evan and Juliette, 47 and 49, have some extra cash for the first time since they were both working full-time and had not yet started their family. What to do with the extra cash? In considering real estate, they sought out a professional real estate investment advisor. In considering securities and the stock market, they sought out a securities investment advisor. They also took a basic class in each type of investment from a national investment firm. After doing this homework, they could make an informed decision about what to do with the extra cash and whom to work with. They have never regretted taking the time to make this investment in themselves and their future.

Personal Consultants

In addition to a financial advisor, you may want and need a personal consultant who can help you establish priorities and create a plan for your retirement and future life. It's my consistent experience that these are two different people with two different skill sets. The person who is a great financial advisor may be great at helping with funding and executing your plan, but probably isn't the best person to help you create it in detail. Conversely, the personal consultant may be great at helping you with your retirement and life planning but probably isn't the best person to be giving you financial advice.

A checklist of criteria for selection of a great personal consultant for your current needs:

- Does he/she walk the talk? Are you reassured by the level of personal planning, execution, and adaptability the personal consultant describes in his/her own professional and personal life? Don't be afraid to ask tough questions and ask for specific examples to know you have solid answers.
- Does the personal consultant have the professional credentials and affiliations that establish him/her as a good choice for you?
- Does the personal consultant have the academic credentials that establish him/her as a highly trained and educated professional in the field? How broadly and thoroughly trained is this person?
- How well networked is this person? Does he/she have the ability and willingness to open some doors for you along the way?

- To what degree is this person a thought leader, well recognized and respected by his/her colleagues? What has this person done to contribute to the advancement of learning and practice in the arena of retirement and life planning? Don't be afraid to ask tough questions about this.
- How much time has this person spent in the workplace and not just as an advisor? What kinds of experiences and challenges did he or she face? If you want someone to be a great advisor for you, you probably want to choose someone whose work life isn't limited to advising only. You don't want someone who can only follow the script as if he/she worked in a call center handling inbound calls.
- What is this person's history of success in working with clients? Remembering that the personal consultant must be measured on the tools, insight, and information provided to clients (since he/she has no control over outcomes), how respected and supported is the personal consultant by his/her current and former clients? Have you been provided with references to check out?
- Do you and this person have enough pure, interpersonal chemistry? How well do you connect with this person? How honest can you be? How well does this person "get" you? How available are you to do your own work supported by this person?

Bill, 56, had been divorced for a long time. He knew that, eventually, he would leave his money to his daughter, Ronnie. In the meantime, he knew he could have 40 years left to live and wanted them to be rewarding ones. He could have started at the financial advisor end of things but instead chose to begin at the personal consultant end because he realized he wanted his life to drive his decisions and financial realities and not the other way around. Bill knew he needed some advice and a well-trained sounding board. He wanted to approach his life from multiple perspectives: professional work, returning to school part-time, what he wanted in an intimate relationship, where and how he wanted to live, and what place Ronnie and the rest of his family would hold in his life. After a lot of discussion with his friends, he concluded this was not going to be about therapy. It was going to be about life planning and the journey that could potentially last for 40 years in a world full of change. Through his weak relationship network, Bill got four recommendations for a personal consultant. The rest was easy. He interviewed all of them and compared them, not to each other, but to the list of selection criteria he had established.

Vera, 77, was recently widowed. Her grandchildren were grown and on their own. Several of her friends were ill or experiencing reduced mobility. In fact, many of them couldn't keep up with Vera anymore. She wanted to do something a bit revolutionary with her life, a promise she had made to her husband—at his request—and to herself when he was so ill. Using her own and her grown children's weak networks, she began her search for the right personal consultant. She ultimately chose a woman about 10 years younger than her, someone who had walked the talk. To her surprise and pleasure, her kids were totally supportive. In many ways, she was modeling future possibilities for them, too.

Regardless of what professional support you are focusing on—financial advisor or personal consultant—find it by asking your strong and weak networks of relationships for professionals whom they or their trusted friends know and respect. Then interview the possible advisors (if you are coupled or married and this is about financial advising, then this should be done by both of you together, and both of you should be involved long term in all conversations about priorities and reviewing performance) to pick among these pre-screened possibilities.

I strongly recommend that you take a hard look at how your financial advisor or personal consultant is compensated for working with you. Make certain you understand the fee structure; review it carefully to see if it is reasonable. Review the ways financial advisors especially can be compensated, such as on an hourly basis, as a percentage of your assets, or on a commission basis. If you choose a commission-based compensation situation, do a thorough review of your progress, status, and costs each year at a minimum. Compare how much you made on your investments with how much your advisor made in handling your account.

In our own case, and after asking our friends who they respected, my wife Linda and I ultimately chose an excellent financial/

securities investment advisor, which met Linda's preference for a woman financial advisor. The choice also met our mutual need to be in a long-term relationship with a professional who is great every day at what we only think about periodically. As often as we are approached and pitched about changing advisors, neither of us has found any good reason to change. I think that's because we did a top job of selection and creating the relationship with her from the beginning.

There is one final way of screening financial advisors and personal consultants: Ask them to tell one or more career-changing stories about themselves. Find out what happened, what they learned, and how they have used the lesson throughout their careers as advisors.

Richard H. Angelotti is a highly accomplished financial professional. He is currently the Chairman/CEO of The Advisory Management Group and has many years of experience in the investing and banking business. Dick told me the cautionary tale—for professional advisors and prospective clients—of a colleague who thought he was great at talking with prospective customers. He and his wife had some social acquaintances who came to see him about handling their investments. When he didn't get the business, he went back to inquire about why. In each case the answer came from the wife of the prospective couple: "We chose someone else because I earned half the money and you talked to my husband the whole time. I was offended." That was a long time ago, but this lesson and story are still important.

Connection to and Relationship with Educational Programs and Organizations

Like it or not, the shelf life of our expertise and skills is growing shorter every day. At work this can look like revolutions in products or services we provide, introduction of technologies that change how business is done, generational and financial shifts that alter who our customers (internal and external) are and what their preferences are. At home this can look like our grandchildren growing into significant capability and independence, our friends retiring but not us or the other way around, the introduction of technologies that allow home surveillance through the Internet, and our readiness to move on to something rather different in our lives. All of these require new skills and knowledge.

You will need to take a hard look at which of your skills/ expertise areas are still current and helpful to you in your life. Also, which are no longer current and/or no longer useful? What new skills and knowledge do you need to just stay current, much less be ahead of the curve? Knowing the answers, you should have in place at least one educational institution or organization. I highly recommend that you have enough experience with it to know how it works, what the rules and policies are, and where you fit in. Some of the faculty or instructors might even be in your weak network of relationships.

There are three major types of programs and organizations to consider:

1. Public university/college/professional associations that can provide you with the applied learning opportunities necessary to keep your skills current for future work or volunteering opportunities
2. So-called lifelong learning programs that can cover the range of content from retirement planning to life-enrichment courses
3. For-profit educational institutions that may or may not convey an academic degree but align their course-work with the emerging skill and expertise needs of employers

Byron retired at age 67 with enough money to sustain his lifestyle until age 84—provided, of course, major medical expenses didn't come along and eat up his nest egg. After six months of leisure he had had it. He knew he didn't want to go back to his old industry. He also knew that he was way too isolated from people age 30 and younger. Byron knew what he wanted and where to get it. He'd been checking it for some time. He decided to go back to school to get certified in the new work he wanted to pursue, which was digital equipment repair. He wanted the challenge. He wanted the work. He wanted to be less generationally isolated. He was by far the oldest in his class. It wasn't an easy course of study but he made it. And he was so happy!

Linda, a youthful 73, plans never to retire. A widow and a grandmother, she likes working part-time. She wants to make up for many of the trade-offs she made when she and Bill were raising their five children. She never studied a foreign language. She knew nothing about opera. Worst of all, in her mind, was that she was still a meat-and-potatoes cook aspiring to be a farm-to-table home chef. Now, she is deeply engaged in a lifelong learning organization, not just as a student but as a part-time volunteer. This isn't about keeping herself busy. It's about fulfillment.

INTANGIBLE ASSETS

Your Own Health

Without your health, retirement and extended life can be limited. What are you actively doing to remain healthy? If you have a health problem now, what are you doing to mitigate or eliminate it? Do you have a physician and a dentist you know and trust from experience? When was your last checkup? What advice did you get and how well have you followed up on it?

William is 53 and Yolanda is 55. He worries about her health and nags her regularly to get a primary care doctor and go for a complete checkup. She worries about his health and nags him regularly about the same thing! This has been going on for more than a decade. They are both lovely people with an immense stubborn streak and huge capacity for avoidance. Thus, neither of them knows the true physical health of either themselves or the other person. Therefore, any retirement extended life planning they do is inevitably missing important components that make what they want more likely to happen.

Unfulfilled but Still Viable and Important Ambitions

Just because you are planning retirement and extended life, you needn't abandon some of the important dreams and ambitions you set aside during the years you were raising kids or building a career or owning a house or continuing to go to school.

Now age 57, Sarah always wanted to be a singer and stage performer. She is a great classroom teacher. She has begun taking singing lessons in the evening. This longtime desire still has power and pleasure for her. She is pursuing being a backstage volunteer at her local Playhouse Theater.

Tom, age 66, wanted to be a long-distance runner. Work, kids, the house, family commitments, going to graduate school at night, travel to customer sites, consistently unavailable regular time slots, and just everyday life intervened. Now retired, or at least not working for the moment, he has begun training with a group of After 65 runners and hopes to run in a marathon late this year. Tom has carried this ambition around for most of his life. It still has power and pleasure for him. And it's not as hopeless as he expected it to be.

Sarah, age 82, has advanced cancer; she has wanted to dance at her granddaughter's wedding since Emily was born. Emily is getting married next month and Sarah has every intention of dancing. Her future may not be long term, but it is still "rich, rich, and rich" as she describes it.

Phil, 55, wants his children to be proud of him. He doesn't much care about what his parents think. He does care about what Cate, his wife, thinks but not as much as the kids. When they were young, he had a big problem with alcohol and it didn't go well. Now, 25 years later, Phil is working on figuring out a way for the kids to be proud of what he's proud about himself. They are all sitting down to talk about it this afternoon.

New Intentions and Ambitions

The freshness of new interests and ambitions can be both bracing and stimulating whether you are planning for or already into retirement as you have defined it for yourself.

Rory, age 73, never dreamed he would get into deep-sea fishing. He didn't grow up near an ocean. He and Beth didn't have their careers or raise their kids near one, either. However, since the two of them moved to a warm, beach-related place, Rory has fallen in love with deep-sea fishing. He has already begun working toward getting a captain's license and is looking at boats. Who knew his "retirement" would look like this?

Sheila and Beth, both 59, persevered for years in their desire to live a "normal" life as the only lesbian couple in the neighborhood. It was rough going sometimes. With the advent of the Supreme Court decision on gay marriage, they feel both more legitimized and supported. They have decided they would never have made it before: Four at a time, they are having their neighbors to dinner at their house. They are beginning to form a new community.

A Secure Sense of Self, Independent of Historic Roles and Responsibilities

Most of us spend the earlier years of our lives knowing who we are through role and performance goals. I'm Fred's daughter. I'm an award-winning athlete. I wanted to play the tuba but got pressured by my mother into the violin; I'm a tuba player wearing a violinist's mask. I'm a parent. I'm a homeowner. I'm a boss and/or an employee. I'm the president of the church council.

Part of the gift of being After 50 is the opportunity to get to know and appreciate ourselves outside of role. We don't have to be role-free. We do have to develop a sense of ourselves beyond roles and goals. Coming to this point is not always easy or comfortable. Sometimes it means we have to slow down enough to acquaint ourselves with ourselves. In the end, the people who are willing to do this work always feel their later lives are additionally satisfying and rich.

Gwen, age 64, loves her grandchildren. She does. But Gramma, like many other roles she still holds, is becoming something that needs to move to a minority position in her life. She's stepping out into things from work to sports to school she never would have considered. The only way she can figure out how to do this is to have her new activities take up much more of her life space, energy, and attention than her roles do. Not all the roles are going away, but she doesn't want to be dominated by them anymore. "I want my own sense of myself," she told me recently. Her husband is her biggest, most active supporter. Her kids aren't happy with it yet.

Curiosity

Curiosity, like health, is something that is easily overlooked until it's gone. What can make childhood wonderful? Curiosity! This applies to retirement and extended life, too.

Shoshana, age 71, couldn't take it anymore. Friends were taking a road trip through new-to-them countryside in a large van they rented together for the purpose. Everyone had expressed an interest in taking this trip. Yet three of the six passengers, all her friends, had spent the last 90 minutes talking without ever looking out the window or expressing interest in the passing scenery. "If you are going to keep talking and not looking, would you mind explaining to me why you came?" she finally asked. "Oh," was the response. "We're perfectly happy to stay home but since you were coming we thought we'd come along and bring our regular conversations with us."

Roy, age 70, took his oldest grandchild, Seth, to museums regularly. It wasn't that he was a museum freak. Roy had spent a lifetime being curious. He simply wanted to pass on to his grandson the habit of curiosity. How did he do this? At every museum they visited, his grandson had to show his grandfather two things that interested him, explain why they had attracted him, and what made him want to understand more about them. Gradually Seth was developing the habit of critical seeing and curiosity.

An example from my own network of relationships: Patricia Bonarek, now in her 70s, is my Sogetsu Ikebana Sensei (instructor) and one of the most fearlessly curious people I know. I interviewed her for an example of how she had put her curiosity to work, living and being a schoolteacher and school principal internationally working for the U.S. Department of Defense.

George: "I started to study the art of Ikebana when I first was transferred to Yokohama, Japan, in 1975. Previously, I had lived and worked in Europe where you could translate a lot of things and read the signs. Suddenly I was a complete illiterate. Exploring the city, I saw a sign in both English and Japanese at the famous old Silk Hotel. The sign said, 'Ikebana, Japanese Floral Design, an Exhibition.' I went in and was extremely impressed because it already was the start of winter in November, but they had used these branches and flowers to make wonderful, temporary works of art. So, I found myself a teacher who only spoke Japanese and I had to draw out everything and figure out what she was saying. Thus, I began my study of Ikebana. After studying Ikebana for three years, I was transferred to the Philippines. Later, I was transferred to Okinawa. I hadn't kept up with my art in those Philippine years, but I wanted to study it again. So, in Okinawa I found for myself a highly respected Ikebana teacher, Betty Hsu, and began taking lessons again, this time in English. My first lesson was probably a big flop because I had not studied for so long. She said to me, 'I want to see how much you have learned and remembered.' Well, the only thing I had remembered was you cut like mad—so I cut everything like mad and I made a mess. There was no way you could salvage this at all. One other student in the class said, 'Ohhh, you didn't measure,' and I thought, 'Oh dear.' Betty could have lost me right then but with her grand 'Oriental Wisdom' and patience she said, 'Oh, Patricia, I see you are not afraid to cut.' This hooked me, and I have studied, practiced, and demonstrated Sogetsu Ikebana around the world ever since. Who knew I would eventually become a retired educator and a high-ranking Sogetsu Ikebana teacher?"

You can learn more about Sogetsu Ikebana and maybe even catch a glimpse of Patricia at http://www.iisarasota.com/boardcommittees.

Courage

Like curiosity, courage can seem intangible, only becoming more solid-seeming when it is practiced. What was the last courageous thing you did? What did you learn from it? If you could do it differently (more wisely), what would you do? Do you think of curiosity and courage as assets of yours?

Julie, 63, was divorced a year ago. She recently went out on a date, her first in 45 years. "It was fun and scary," she reported afterwards. "And I'm glad I didn't chicken out the way I thought I might. I'll probably do it again."

Bonnie, 70, a retired nurse, has had an idea for a medical instrument for a long time. "No one is going to take me seriously at this age," she said. Her friends pressured her into making an appointment with a local start-up business incubator. Suddenly she was exposed to an entire network of experts. Instead of feeling foolish, she clearly was an expert with both skill and knowledge that none of the others—experts in different disciplines—had. "Whether it turns into something or not down the road," she said, "I was so afraid that I couldn't not go. I hope it turns into something and I can find my place in it."

Mike, now 72, has been a freewheeling, constantly in-motion entrepreneur since he was 15. He has made a lot of money, mostly through creating total business successes and some real disasters of businesses, too. This meant, among other things, that he missed a lot of his kids growing up. At the moment, he is facing his biggest fear: living a much smaller life than he has ever been willing to live before. He owes it to his wife, Mary, and to himself in his opinion. Adrenalin is a powerful drug to be addicted to, especially if it's laced with testosterone. He is facing his previous archenemy, calmness. He knows that to win this time he's going to have to surrender, and that is taking courage.

Your Current Skills

Make a comprehensive list of what you know how to do. From that list itemize the skills you must have to do it. Don't skimp on this part of the inventory. I know this is work, but it's a lot less work than trying to operate in the world without knowing what your skills are. How can you explain it to someone else if you can't name it for yourself?

Unlike her husband, Naomi, 71, always had a knack for working with people. He had retired to become a serious golfer. She didn't want to retire and still doesn't. This was a source of some friction in the beginning because he wanted her to be available to do things together at any hour. They compromised. She went from full-time to two-thirds time at her job as a concierge at a major hotel in order to be more available to him. He, historically a non-joiner, went out of his way to join three different Men's Golf Leagues to develop new possibilities and lessen the pressure he had put on his wife to be more available. Now it's Naomi's and his expectation that no matter what happens as they plan a future, her people skills will play an important role for her and for them.

What are you good at that you like? What are the skills necessary to do it well?

What are you good at that you don't much like? What are the skills necessary to do it well?

Your Current Knowledge/Expertise

What do you see as your areas of expertise? How long have you had this knowledge? Where did it come from? How current is it? How do you use it to advantage? Don't skimp on this part of the inventory. I know this is work, but it's a lot less work than trying to operate in the world without knowing what your knowledge and expertise are. How can you explain it to someone else if you can't name it for yourself?

Mack, 81, started out as a boy fixing cars. He just had that knack for looking at something and figuring it out. It grew rapidly as neighbors asked him to look at everything from toasters to lawn mowers. It gave him a lot of satisfaction. During his long career as a fireman, he pretty much set this knowledge aside. However, as he approaches the notion of retiring, he has gone back to school to transform both his approach to and understanding of repairs. It's his hope that eventually he can once again be Mr. Fixit in his sprawling neighborhood.

What do you know a lot about, deeply, that you really like?

What do you know a lot about, deeply, that you don't much like?

IT'S TIME TO GO TO WORK:
LIST AND EVALUATE YOUR OWN ASSETS

It's time for you to do a thoughtful, thorough analysis of the condition of these assets in your own life AND their sufficiency for you to go where you want to go. Once again, if you are coupled or married, you should both do this together or at least individually and share the information in detail.

Reader Exercise

1. Draw a vertical line down the center of several sheets of paper or create a Word or other document that serves the same purpose.
2. In the left column, place the entire list of assets.
3. In the right column, be prepared to place your assessment of: a) the sufficiency of your assets now, b) their sufficiency to support the future you imagine for you right now, and c) what needs to be done to shore up or replace those that don't or won't meet your need. Allow plenty of room in the right column.
4. Write a report for yourself that captures the important information from your work and lays it out in a coherent fashion.
5. Share the information with your spouse. Your spouse should be doing this and share his/her information with you.

Note: This will take time. It doesn't have to be done alone. If you don't know the answers or don't trust your own answers, you can go to someone whom you respect and ask him or her what answers he or she would give for you.

Hint: Pick someone you respect who is perceptive, candid, and not so close to you that the feedback to you will be diluted. If you can't think of someone, ask one of your friends for a recommendation and to open the connection door for you.

Do the assessment in manageable bites. If you rush through to completion, the end product will show that. If you do only partial work or never complete it, the product will show that, too.

This approach will capture and paint for you a complex and complete assessment of where you are right now. It's the inventory count that's accurate and outstandingly informative for you and your plan. This—taking inventory of where we are—is consistently the most solid place to start retirement or life planning.

IMAGINING YOUR FUTURE

Now that you have completed your Asset Inventory, we can move on to Imagining Your Future. We are going to use the three-perspective approach again that we worked with earlier in the book.

This is because, given the current revolution in planning, we can have long-term intentions but true long-term planning (with the expectation that we have the necessary information, know what success will look like, and can execute a stable plan on an unmoving field of permanent terrain) is unlikely at best. You will need to imagine your future from these three distances or perspectives and then build the best-fit plan for you.

THE NEXT 12 TO 18 MONTHS

Let's begin with the near-term perspective.

- In the next 12 to 18 months, what would you like to have happen in your life? Think about it, write it down, interview some others (keep the HINT from the previous reader exercise in mind when deciding who to interview).
- In the next 12 to 18 months, what would you like to be true of you? Ditto on the instructions.
- What goals and time frames do you want to set for your life and for yourself that, through achievement, would assure successful achievement?

It's my experience that the first attempts at this are usually drafts that serve as the basis for the eventual picture of what you would like to be true of your life in this 12-to-18-month time frame.

THE 18-MONTH TO 48-MONTH TIME FRAME

Let's move on to the middle-term perspective.

- In the following 18 to 48 months, what would you like to be true and have happen in your life? Think about it, write it down, and interview some others (keep the HINT in mind as you decide who to interview).

- In the following 18 to 48 months, what would you like to be true of you? Ditto on the instructions.
- What goals and time frames do you want to set for your life and for yourself that, through achievement, would assure successful achievement?

It's my experience that the first attempts at this are usually drafts that serve as the basis for the eventual picture of what you would like to be true of your life in this 18-to-48-month time frame.

Caution: The further from today your preferences are, the more likely they are to morph or need to be updated because of new information, experiences, and altered preferences. It's very important to note that your imagination for this period is expressed in terms of preferences, not guarantees or total failure on your part if things change.

THE 48-MONTH TO 96-MONTH TIME FRAME

Let's move on to the longer-term perspective.

- In the following 48 to 96 months, what would you like to be true of and have happen in your life? Think about it, write it down, and interview some others (keep the earlier HINT in mind as you decide who to interview).
- In the following 48 to 96 months, what would you like to be true of you? Ditto on the instructions.
- What goals and time frames do you want to set for your life and for yourself that, through achievement, would assure successful achievement?

It's my experience that the first attempts at this are usually drafts that serve as the basis for the eventual picture of what you would like to be true of your life in this 48-to-96-month time frame.

Caution: The further in the future from today your preferences are, the more likely they are to morph or need to be updated because of new information, experiences, and altered preferences. It's very important to note that your imagination for this period is best expressed in terms of intentions, not guarantees or total failure on your part if things change.

In the final diagnosis, great plans are no longer plans that are linear, inviolable, run across steady, stable time periods and terrain, or measured for success in terms of flawless execution.

Great plans today are incremental, involve at least three time perspectives, are living/breathing documents that sit on our shoulders talking to us, and, most important, need to be adapted regularly in the face of new information. What makes this all go particularly well is our own accompanying willingness to adapt ourselves along with the plan.

Reader Exercise

1. Draw a vertical line down the center of several sheets of paper or create a Word or other document that serves the same purpose.
2. In the left column, place your 12-to-18-month, 18-to-48-month, and 48-to-96-month goals/preferences/intentions/priorities.
3. In the right column, be prepared to place the assets (tangible, intangible knowledge, and skills) that you already have and that you will need for each goal/preference/intention/priority for each perspective/period of time. Where there is a great match between goals and assets, acknowledge that and celebrate. Where there are gaps between goals and assets, acknowledge that, too, and make some notes in the margin about possible remedies for the gaps. If you have no gaps, there is a good possibility you are only working with what is comfortable for you now. You may be cutting yourself off from a richer future than you originally imagined.
4. Share the information with your spouse. Your spouse should be doing this same exercise and sharing his/her own information with you.

Note: This will take time. It doesn't have to be done alone. If you don't know the answers or links or don't trust your own answers or links, you can go to someone you respect and ask him/her what answers he/she would give for you.

Hint: Pick someone you respect who is perceptive, candid, and not so close to you that the feedback to you will be diluted. If you can't think of someone, ask one of your friends for a recommendation and to open the connection door for you.

Do this work in manageable bites. If you rush through to completion, the end product will show that. If you do only partial work or never complete it, the product will show that, too.

This approach will capture and paint for you a penetrating and complete assessment of where you want to go and what you currently have in place to help you do that.

BEGINNING TO PULL IT ALL TOGETHER

You've done a great job by now of aligning your short-, mid-, and long-term goals/preferences with the assets you have in place.

My friend and colleague Andrea Gallagher, 57, is president of Senior Concerns in Southern California. She is a certified senior advisor (CSA) and founder of Rethinking Your Future™. Andrea is a past president of Life Planning Network and she served as Life Transitions Chair of the International Conferences on Positive Aging. Andrea can be reached at https://www.seniorconcerns.org/author/andrea.

In our interview, we talked about planning in increments.

George: What do you think of planning in increments?

Andrea: At 57, I don't think it necessarily does me a whole lot of good to be thinking and worrying about what's going to happen when I am 90. Except, of course, for giving some thought to financial and legal planning. I think what's important for me is to look in shorter horizons. You know, I've reinvented myself once and I am sure I will do it again at least one more time. My focus is often on how I can have purpose and contribute in the stage of planning that I'm in. When my husband and I went to revise our estate planning, an attorney I know well decided to write that we'd both want to live as long as possible in our current house if one or the other of us passes away. I said, I'm a social being so I know that I would be absolutely miserable in a house all by myself even if I had a caregiver caring for me. That would not sing to my heart. So, my instruction was to certainly not put that in our documents. It's way too soon for me to know what the best arrangement will be then.

By now, I hope you can see where the strong alignments are between where you want to go and the assets you have.

I also hope you can begin to see where you want to go with a clearer, more strategic eye and the places where your assets are complete or need renewal, replacement, or creation from scratch.

If that's where you are, we're ready to move on to Essential Questions You Need to Ask and Answer in the next chapter. If you aren't there yet, go back and review/complete the work until you are. And, once again, you don't have to do this alone. It often helps to do it with a well-chosen friend or relative.

chapter 5

Essential Questions
You Need to Ask and Answer

A re you working with a financial professional and do you know what assets you have and whether they're growing to keep up with your future plans? Are you keeping your financial circumstances in mind without letting them dominate the asset review you have been working on here? Are you able to use your newly acquired and updated sense of ALL your assets into formulating the crucial questions you can be asking right now and getting the answers you need?

It would be so much easier if you could ask five universal, all-encompassing, permanent questions to obtain all the key answers you need to plan for your future.

However, the reality, as you know from your own life and our conversation so far in this book, is that while we share similar concerns with our family and friends, in the end retirement planning and life planning are as individual as shoes. Your preferences in terms of style, purpose, durability, fit, comfort, price, compatibility, fashion, materials, quality, design, and availability are likely to be different from those of your partner or next-door neighbor.

It would also be easier if the questions stayed constant across our lives AND the answers, as well as the plan, were permanent.

The reality is, unfortunately, that both the questions and the answers change periodically as life unfolds and time passes. You already know this at some level if you have ever been divorced, lost a job, buried a parent, changed careers, lived with trying teenagers, returned to school later in life, moved across town/the state/the country, or had a moment of artistic or nature-driven recognition—whether visual or auditory or tactile—that somehow changed you forever.

I'm going to give you questions to ask of yourself and others with the understanding that this is not meant to be a specific map or a checklist. The quality of the questions and the sufficiency of their answers to the degree possible are, in the end, up to you.

You are discovering here a revolutionary way to understand and build a modern retirement or life plan rooted in the realities of our present and our potential future, not in our own past or the past of others.

The quality of the question always drives the quality of the answer (I've said that before and you'll hear it again).

Here are four major clues that will help you understand whether superior or inferior questions are being asked:

1. Does the perspective of the question match the situation? If it's a big-picture situation and a little, tiny, detail-oriented question—or vice versa—especially one that can be answered yes or no, something is wrong. Perspective is important.

2. Is the question designed to distract and derail the questioner (and the audience) in order to avoid a particular subject?

3. Does the answer to the question in any way assign blame to someone else as a first step such as, "Who made this mess?"

4. Does the question represent a sincere effort to discover alternatives, answers, and possibilities not yet known?

Part of what I do for a living is to upgrade the quality of the questions being asked by my clients (individuals, couples, small to medium-sized businesses, and divisions of large businesses) so that the answer gives the highest-quality information and insight possible. This in turn leads to stronger strategy, a superior balance of planning and action, and increases the chance of success in retirement and in life.

It sounds easy. It isn't.

PAULA AND JEREMIAH

Paula and Jeremiah came to see me about Paula changing careers. Recently, she had unexpectedly lost her long-term job and was angry, hurt, frightened, and didn't know where to start. All she knew for certain was that she didn't want to stay in the same industry. The question that consumed her was, "Why is this happening to me?" And that was pretty much all she could think about at the time. Jeremiah was there to support her but he didn't get to say much.

Of course she was hurt and angry, but mostly she was embarrassed. Consider the four clues above. Then take a look at Paula's question. Not only was the perspective disconnected from the situation, the question was, too. The question was not a sincere effort to gather key data. And I suspect the question she was asking was the first step on the path to transfer of blame. That's a very low-quality question, indeed.

Acknowledging wholeheartedly that she deserved a reasonable time to grieve, I asked her to estimate how long that would take and to make an appointment for them to return to me and work on much better questions and answers.

Upon their return, the three of us worked together on her better questions. These turned out to be:

1. What would I like the next years of my life to be like?
2. How does work fit into that?
3. What are the best-fit work possibilities?
4. How do I get there from here?

This opened the door to holding the right perspectives and getting necessary information upon which action planning could be built.

Recently, a pre-retirement couple, Kayla and Dion, came to see me for advice. His single question was, "When can I retire?" Her single question was, "What can he find to do so that he isn't in my hair all the time?" She didn't want to be his one-woman, post-retirement entertainment committee and captive companion.

I asked them if they could set aside their questions for now and individually review their assets (see Chapter 4) as a place to start, coming back together to share their reviews with each other afterward. Dion jumped on the exercise. For him, some action, any action, was better than what he described as his "passive suffering." Kayla was much more reluctant to review her assets. She hadn't worked since the kids were born, now long ago, and thought of herself as not qualified to have assets that could be reviewed. I carefully explained that work didn't necessarily mean outside employment. She had worked hard all those years running a household and being involved in the community. She had been building assets all the while. She just hadn't thought about them that way until now. Think of how capable a CEO it takes to run an entire complex household and lifestyle, complete with four growing kids, making it look easy and graceful! How could she look me in the eye and say she didn't have assets when, in fact, many of hers could be of equal or greater value to them in retirement and life planning than Dion's were?

Tucking this revolutionary idea under her arm and marching out of my office with her husband to do her own asset review, she seemed to walk differently.

Kayla and Dion returned to meet with me two weeks later. Dion had given up all intentions of retiring, telling me, "I'm not in a financial or asset position to simply stop working. And on top of that, now that I've taken a hard look at my assets, I can see several of them have fallen in to neglect through my inattention. This feels renewing to me. How about working on a life plan instead of limiting our work to retirement?" Kayla said, "To my surprise, I now want to go to work part-time. It's been so many years since I brought earnings into the household. On top of that, I can see that I've been under-stimulated and coasting. I deserve better than that and have already talked to a friend who runs a large shop about going to work for her three days a week. We both think it looks like a good fit, for her and me. I'm with Dion now. May we work on a life plan instead of focusing on retirement? We really want to take a look at our future and our assets."

SPEAKING OF THE FUTURE AND SUPERIOR QUESTIONS

I admit it. We haven't focused much on the future yet. Why is this? It's because I firmly believe in getting a full and accurate take of our current assets, knowledge, and skills first. It's very important to imagine a great, evolving future for yourself, provided you are imagining in reasonable time segments and not in one big, sprawling, long-term picture.

As we begin, what are some critical questions you should be asking yourself about your future?

1. What is a reasonable planning horizon for you?
2. What would you like to be the major elements of your life within that time horizon?
3. What would a representative day look like?
4. How much private time will you need regularly?
5. What would be the primary differences between your life now and the life you imagine?
6. If you are sharing a plan with a significant other, are you on the same page, having mutual clarity about common intentions?
7. If you are sharing a plan with a significant other, do you have enough space/mutual support and commitment for your individually different intentions, too?
8. What kinds of people and companionship will you need and want in your life? How many will be sufficient? What would characterize the interactions and connections?
9. Ideally, where would you live?
10. What are the features and amenities you will need in your immediate environment and community, wherever you are?

11. What do you need to let go of now with appreciation and leave by the side of the road as you move on because, no matter how useful it was in the past, it won't be in the future?

12. What are the most likely variables that could cause you to have to adapt yourselves or the plan or both?

13. Who else needs to understand and support your plan and action steps?

14. What personal goals are you setting for yourself as part of your plan's execution and for a richer life of your own?

15. Where would you start?

16. What steps would you have to take?

17. What is the risk of what you are considering?

18. What is the benefit of what you are considering?

19. How prepared are you really to have something throw a wrench into the plan so you have to adapt both the plan and yourself?

Terri and Devin were anxious to get going on their future. Retirement was a year away. The pressure to anticipate and plan was enormous. They felt as if they had to "get it right" immediately without time for transition and learning and successes and mistakes.

How many of us have been there, too, at various points in our lives?

They were especially anxious to get some breathing room, free of the responsibility of the last of their kids, jobs, home maintenance, employees, volunteer activities, and work-related travel. They had spent a lot of their lives taking care of others. Now it was their turn and they had to get it right!

If they had come to you for advice, what questions would you have asked them?

Mine were:

1. What would "right" look like? How will you know?

2. What would "really good" look like and how would it differ from "right"?

3. What is the cost to you of "right" versus "really good"?

Anthony, age 77 and a widower came to see me about creating a life plan. Having lived to that age and being in great health, he understood that, statistically at least, he was more likely than average to live quite a while longer. "I'm planning on 94," he said. That gives me a 17-year planning horizon. I know enough about your work with my friends to know that I should be crafting a five-year, extendable/adaptable plan and not a huge road-map-style plan directly from here to 94 with no allowance for bumps in the road, hairpin turns, or refueling stations. Where do we start?"

He was ready to look at his future. Anthony wasn't afraid of tough questions. He had already done a full and penetrating asset review.

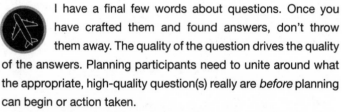 I have a final few words about questions. Once you have crafted them and found answers, don't throw them away. The quality of the question drives the quality of the answers. Planning participants need to unite around what the appropriate, high-quality question(s) really are *before* planning can begin or action taken.

Great questions that were part of formulating the plan can and should be asked regularly as reality checks and to see changes, both continuous and discontinuous. The list of best questions may be a living, breathing part of your imagining and acting upon your future. Some questions may remain. Some may fall away to be replaced by now-relevant others. It's OK for the questions to evolve as your life and plan does.

Make sure that informed answers are a part of a larger pattern of going toward something as opposed to away from it. If the questions are selected and the answers chosen primarily around no, not, or moving away from something, this is an indicator of something that isn't really about crafting a life After 50. It's about escape. Escape may be essential as an interim stage but it doesn't do well as an imagined life in the long run.

chapter 6

Knowledge and Skills
You Need Along the Way

Navigating the uncertain takes planning as you've learned in earlier chapters. All the plans are predicated on your ability (and willingness) to pay attention, think, articulate, and learn.

In my own case, I frequently feel inarticulate and a bit like someone from another galaxy when I visit the modern/contemporary art of the wonderful new Whitney Museum in New York; yet I am completely at home and entranced in the museum's new building itself. In that case architecture speaks to me more loudly than pieces of art. By contrast, I am fully at home and connected to the portraiture and other art in the Smithsonian's National Portrait Gallery in Washington D.C., yet I am usually oblivious to the building itself. How about you? What most regularly draws and keeps your attention? What are the most representative of your daily thoughts? Which have the most impact on you and others? In which situations do you feel most and least able to articulate? How aware are you that learning is truly a lifelong process?

Five-year-old Irwin was on his first sleepover at his friend Billy's house. In the middle of the night he awoke crying. Billy's mother came to comfort him and asked him what was the matter. Through his tears Irwin said, "I didn't know it would be so much darker at night at your house than it is at mine."

Kelly, age 12, was wildly enthusiastic throughout the religious holidays. Suddenly she was glum. Her dad came to check on her. "Why," she asked plaintively, "does time go so much faster when we're happiest?"

Christopher, age 21, was about to graduate from college, the first in his family to do so. "What are you going to do now?" asked his grandmother. "I'm not sure," he said. "My whole life has been about getting good grades and graduating. I don't think I know, yet, how to live any other kind of life."

Maria was 40 years old and her daughter, Manuela, was 17. "I had the teenage girl mood swings, too, Manuela. It felt totally out of control for me, too. And I never did figure out what stopped or started them other than hormones. I still don't know. I just had to ride it out, like being in tall waves, until they finally flattened out. I wish I had an answer for you but I don't."

Martin, age 63, and Andrea, age 61, had been married for 41 years. During that time, they both had jobs, went to school at night, raised five kids, supported their church, took care of both sets of aging parents, participated in community and volunteer activities, and completed the hundreds of tasks it takes to keep such a life together. At breakfast one morning Andrea said, "I've been noticing that all these years we've been like two horses in parallel harness, pulling whatever was the day's load. Usually it was about what other people needed and our roles in making that happen. Along the way we stopped talking; we were such a good team together that we didn't need to. This Retirement Thing is starting to scare me. For the first time we're going into unfamiliar territory where we have few examples. We can't afford to not work at all. We are both tired of demanding more-than-full-time jobs and ready to be done with that. I don't think we know what our options are. We're going to have to start talking with each other again and differently. That's scaring me, too. Do you think we can do it?".

Eighty-four-year-old George was really sick for the first time in his life. He looked up at his family from his hospital bed and said, "If I had known I was going to live this long, I would have taken better care of myself."

Lollie, age 101, loved to sit in a rocking chair on the porch where she lived. Her 21-year-old great, great granddaughter, sitting in the adjacent rocker, had just asked Lollie about the secret to living so long. Said Lollie, "Don't smoke, a thimble of the best bourbon every day, and kiss and hug as often as possible. That's what worked for me. I don't know what will work for you, sweetheart."

Raise your hand if at any point in your life so far you already had all the skills and expertise you needed to last for the rest of your life. Anyone?

Raise your hand if at some point in your life a change came along, either chosen by you or imposed on you without permission, and you found you had to scramble to figure out what to do because previous experience hadn't perfectly prepared you for that moment. Everyone, right?

Raise your hand if you already know that the language and images you have to work with regarding both retirement planning and life planning are currently inadequate to the total task of After 50 imagining, planning, action, and adapting because so much has changed that the word "retirement" is no longer adequate for the many possibilities, situations, and needs. Do I see a sprinkling of hands?

In our society and educational systems, it's my experience that for the most part someone in authority identifies what we don't know but need to learn, creates a curriculum and syllabus, and we proceed to learn it and pass the test. Of course, we write papers and conduct experiments, among other activities, but the crowning evidence of our success is our test scores. In my opinion, this has led to an exaggerated focus on passing the test, solving the problem, and our strong, national bias for action over reflection.

THE IMPORTANCE—AND SOMETIMES INADEQUACY—OF OUR WORDS

As human beings one of the ways we communicate is through words, which are really symbols that allow us to think and speak and our listeners to hear and interpret for themselves. Without these symbols and fluency in them, we are rendered both inarticulate and isolated as if we were suddenly transported to another planet with an alien language and culture.

Some of these words are written. Think stop sign, poetry, meatloaf recipe, love letter, news headlines on your smartphone or tablet, and receipt for dry cleaning.

Some of these words are spoken. Think election campaign speeches, family meeting conversations, news broadcasts, an elevator that tells you what floor you have reached, and commercials on TV and the Internet.

We use lots of other symbols such as facial expressions, open or closed doors, images, music, and gestures to communicate, of course. These all combine with our word usage to form our daily language.

But for our purposes, I'll stick to words. Our interpretations of word symbols can vary wildly. Some of them are images such as photos and other forms of art and visual commerce.

Here are six examples of how our language symbols have failed to keep up with or stay ahead of current realities and usage:

1. *Job.* A form of work for pay in which the employer and employee agree that in exchange for skills and performance within certain hours at certain locations, a permanent or semi-permanent arrangement is created. We have failed to craft language that matches the emerging reality of work for pay. For all the hoopla about the number of jobs created (which seldom mentions whether or not they pay enough to keep a middle-class family afloat), the fact is that we are leaving the purely job-dominated era and moving toward freelancing, self-employment, entrepreneurial work, project-based work, and other forms of work for pay that may end up challenging jobs for preeminence sooner than we expect.

2. *Family.* Mom or Grandma, Dad or Grandpa, the kids, Fido the dog and Fluffy the cat. Despite overwhelming statistics to the contrary, many of us still consider any configuration, that is different unqualified to be a family. We don't have a word for what that other configuration is, but it isn't a family to many of us. Our language has failed to keep up with the new, already well-established norms of our country.

3. *Retirement.* A later period of life based on a previous extended work life, which, through programs, fully funded the ability to not work at all for the rest of our lives. We have failed to create language that matches the emerging reality of retirement: "retiring" much later, the necessity to keep working, taking a job to get health-care coverage and other benefits that are more important than the actual compensation, leaving full-time employment to buy into a business or start a venture or accept other full- and part-time employment. Retirement is no longer the broadly shared golden dream of yore.

4. *Permanent.* We have failed to create language that matches the current truth about levels of change. We're still talking Career Path in a world in which work is continually being reinvented, departments and companies come and disappear and reorganize with amazing regularity, and leadership is an increasingly distributed function. Long-term employment is no longer universally a guarantee of respect, admiration, and wisdom. In fact, permanent or long-term employment can now be seen as a measure of a lack of ambition and adaptability.

5. *Elderly.* We have failed to create language that adequately grasps sophistication about aging beyond chronological age. When is "elderly"? What are the criteria? How can one 80-year-old person seem elderly while someone else the exact same age is obviously not? How can someone age 65 seem really old and his uncle so young at age 78? It isn't that we need to drop the term elderly. It's that we need to understand what we mean when we use it and create additional language that captures the nuances of aging today. Otherwise we simply have an inaccurate category into which to throw most people, ourselves included, over a certain age.

6. *Plan.* We have failed to create language that matches the reality of short-term, adaptable planning in contrast to long-term, map-like plans. Why is this important? Because when it comes to After 50, planning is an essential but very different exercise and awareness than it was in the days when you created a plan, put it in a drawer, and pulled it out a few years later to use as a basis for a new plan.

Reader Exercise

Before moving on, let's practice with the following exercise that explores the power and weakness of words. You should read and discuss this section in a group of, at a minimum, two people, but ideally four or five.

What do these words "say" to you? What do you say to yourselves about them upon contact? Show them to others and ask what they "hear" and imagine in the following.

- *"Retirement is the natural and God-given right of every man and woman past the age of 65."*   *—Anonymous*

- *"Go to the store and buy enough food to feed everyone."*   *—Desperate Mother to her daughter*

- *"The quality of the question drives the quality of the answer."*   *—George Schofield*

- *"Remember, George, I am your personal physician and not the Health Police."*   *—My doctor, John Collins*

- *"When I see that canvas hanging on the wall covered in yellow paint with no other distinguishing features, I keep waiting for the artist to come back and finish it. What am I missing?"*   *—Exasperated museumgoer*

What are the words you use regularly whose meaning and usage are now much larger and more diversified than in the past?

FOCUS ON LEARNING, NOT JUST ACQUIRING A LIST OF THINGS YOU HAVE MEMORIZED

I'm convinced that when it comes to learning, knowledge, and skills, many, if not the majority, of us go straight to memorization and repetition, passing the test or solving the problem, and moving on to the next item in our attention queue. Eventually we can even come to assume that our previous experiences and solutions will automatically apply to and resolve our current and upcoming situations.

Earlier in this book, I distinguished between knowledge and skills. In truth it takes both because having the skill without the knowledge means we can mechanically act but fail to grasp any of the strategic importance or implications of what we are doing and why. Conversely, having the knowledge without the skill means we can understand but not act effectively in our own or others' best interest.

Memorization and repetition as skills are very important and valid. As a primary method they work in an environment where everything is stable and reasonably unmoving. And they don't necessarily guarantee understanding.

Primary reliance on memorization and repetition will be at odds with the world many of us are entering or will face in the future when we are doing our planning for retirement and life. I am endeavoring here to point out that adaptability and life pioneering may not come with familiar tools and we will have to seek them out. See Chapter 2, "Today's New 50-plus Lives," and also Chapter 3, "A Tour of the New Normal."

The following are my recommendations for understanding and skills, but it is not meant to be all-inclusive or a complete checklist of everything you will need. Instead, I hope you will use it as a smart and strategic foundation upon which you can build all of the additional understanding and skills you will discover you need as you go along.

MY TOP 9 RECOMMENDATIONS FOR THE MOST IMPORTANT KNOWLEDGE AND SKILLS

KNOWLEDGE #1

All the types of content expertise required for you to be executive director of your After 50 life. We have discussed many of these throughout your life.

Skill Set: Everything it takes for full, active responsibility to plan, craft, adapt, and live your high-quality life After 50.

Phoebe, 62, had led a very successful life: bank VP, gourmet cook, grown kids, education, husband, and travel. When Bill announced he had found someone else and wanted a divorce, she was shocked. True, they hadn't been getting along the way they used to, but for it to come to this now? "OK," she eventually thought, "I've got to get my act together here and plan for myself."

She immediately made two discoveries: 1) She was poor at planning for herself based on her unique needs and preferences. She had always built plans based on her family. 2) She had led a life of structures—everything that came with structured work, structured family responsibilities, structured weekends, and the repetition and patterns that performing in multiple roles for a long time can induce. She had no experience creating her own structures from scratch. Because her background was institutional banking and she was used to job descriptions, she decided to write one for herself as executive director of her life. This is what she came up with:

Under the direction and guidance of the Board of Directors (herself), the person in this position (Phoebe) is responsible for the planning, organizing, motivating, assessment, and directing the organization (Phoebe) for maximum effectiveness, satisfaction, and engagement with life. While the incumbent is free to aid and support others, at no time should their priorities indefinitely swamp her own. At no point, unless she is no longer able to do so, will she ask or expect anyone to take more responsibility for her and for her life than she does. She is responsible for all of her own retirement and life planning, although she may employ professional advisors as required. This person must have the ability to communicate effectively with diverse groups, knowledge of budgeting and bookkeeping, life program development, strategic and tactical planning in two- to three-year increments, and both program and overall effectiveness evaluation. She must be able to operate effectively as a single woman, a highly competent person After 50. She will also have the ability to maintain, renew, and upgrade networks of friends and contacts. She may also, according to current demands, from time to time be called upon to be the Chief Financial Officer, Chief Health Officer, Chief Marketing Communications Officer, Chief Materials Procurement Officer, the cook, chauffeur, and janitor. She must have reasonable curiosity and taste for adventure. Finally, she is responsible for forming a Board of Directors (her four closest friends) and holding a board meeting (dinner at her house—she would cook) where she will present to the board members evidence of performance and need for improvement in each of the items mentioned previously in this job description In this way, she will have ritualized having the important conversations regularly AND not become inadvertently isolated. Semi-annually she will be responsible for reporting to the board on her learnings about:

1. What she already knows that applies
2. What she realizes she must learn about
3. Her plan (with time-frame commitments) for items 1 and 2.

And also she is responsible for . . .

4. Updating this position description every six months, or more often, as required.

At least once a month she will have dinner with one or more people, ahead of her in the retirement/life process, whom she respects and admires. The dinner conversation must include high-quality questions about how they got to where they are, what they wish they had known earlier, what they would do differently, what has come as a pleasant surprise, and how they are planning their future. Finally, she must be able to adapt appropriately when things don't go according to plan and reconsider/update the plan and herself as a result.

KNOWLEDGE #2

How to recognize and work with all forms of change from continuous to discontinuous.

Skill Set: Paying close attention, asking great questions, creativity and curiosity, asking for assistance from the right people at the right times, updating plans, staying cool, and personal adaptability.

Barry, age 60, fell off a horse and was badly injured. He was unable to return to work for more than a year. In that time his employer had been acquired by another company, the local office in which he had worked was dramatically downsized, and technologies had been brought in to replace a significant percentage of what Barry and his colleagues used to do. Clearly the company would have a job for him but not his old job that didn't exist anymore. The injury and the acquisition of his employer Barry saw as Continuous Change. The injury and elimination of his job Barry saw as Discontinuous Change. "I'm too young to retire," he said. "How much can you pay me for part-time work, where are the new jobs with the company, and what does your tuition reimbursement cover? I think I want to go back for retraining."

KNOWLEDGE #3

Periodic, effective assessment of your professional and personal networks of the right connections. What do you need? Where are you oversubscribed? Where do you have holes? What do you need to do about it and how soon? How do your networks fit into your plan?

Skill Set: The actual work of building and maintaining networks of relationships: connecting, effective use of technologies and personal time, nurturing, exchanging value over time, requesting, balancing your time and energy among your various networks.

Rafael and Paloma, now ages 71 and 72, respectively, had lived in a large house on a tree-lined, old neighborhood street near the center of the city for years. Both had had big-time careers. The last of the kids had finally left. Paloma and Rafael knew that the big house was a magnet for their twenty-something kids. Eleven years ago, they hit on the perfect solution: retire, sell the big house, and buy a much smaller one in an After 50s community about two hours away in the rolling countryside. Golf. Tennis. Swimming. Shared Interest Clubs. All yards maintained by the homeowners' association. When they moved in, just about everyone was in the same age group and had comparable, shared enthusiasms. Slowly their personal and professional networks in the city began to erode. Lots of people began to retire and two hours each way was too far to drive for a dinner or a lunch. Their network base slowly moved from work-related connections in the city to retirement-related connections in their retirement community. To their surprise, even though they think they are still very young in their early 70s, they began to see several of their neighbors begin to get sick or move to be closer to their kids or withdraw from many of the activities the community provided. Paloma and Rafael were faced with a challenge: In the face of erosion of both their professional and personal networks, where were they going to go or replace people to keep the networks fresh and vital? And what would it take to do that?

KNOWLEDGE #4

Remaining reasonably current in technologies and related awareness.

Skill Set: It isn't that you or I need to know everything about everything technical AND keep our knowledge leading-edge current. However, if we can't speak the language and understand what is still prevalent and what is emerging as hot, it will put us straight out of the conversation and leave us behind.

"I don't own a cell phone," Rick, age 66, the auto salesperson said proudly. "I want my grandkids to talk to me, not text me." I must admit to having some empathy with that. "My job," he continued, "is to have great relationships with my customers. I can outsource to one of my colleagues anytime the introduction of new car owners to all the techie possibilities that await them on the dashboard." "If you don't know what you are selling—features and benefits—why would someone buy from you instead of from someone else?" I asked. "My customers come back to me because they trust me, plain and simple," he said. "What happens when all your current customers are dead and the only salespeople the new customers will want to see are the ones who can talk about the whole car, technologies included?" His response: "I guess that's when I'll have to retire."

KNOWLEDGE #5

How to balance external validation from roles and goals with internal, grounded, and informed validation you provide to yourself.

Skill Set: As we age, many of us will experience our abilities gradually diminishing. Early on it can look like dropping the occasional, very familiar word out of the blue and not be a big deal at all. Much later it can look like greatly reduced memory or tolerance for chaos or mobility. Not all of us will suffer from the same things, of course, and some won't at all, but for the majority of us it will, inevitably, be something. As things happen, our self-esteem can begin to plummet. Most of us have led lives of significant external validation from roles and achievement. Professional: We were a sports champion. Personal: We were known among our friends as the Thoughtful One, never forgetting birthdays. Family: We were always someone's father or mother or granddaughter or sibling or aunt or nephew. If we were good at it, things worked in our favor. If not?

What's my point? My point is that, as we age, even though we feel younger than our chronological age number, we will have decreasing opportunity to garner our self-esteem exclusively from our accomplishments and roles. Either we will have to make do with less OR we will have to learn to build our own self-esteem outside of roles and accomplishments. For many of us, this is a totally revolutionary and counterintuitive idea. We're used to roles and problems and solutions and achievements and goals and more achievements. What else could we need?

Saul, age 68, advertised himself as a "retired salesman and proud of it." His 70-year-old wife, Mimi, wanted him to slow down. He couldn't. In retirement he was still looking for the next challenge, the next mountain to conquer, the next sale to make, and the next card game to win. It reminded Mimi of the days when he was on the roller coaster at work: He was only as good and as valuable as his sales numbers for last month, his most recent accomplishment. His ongoing search for Next regularly exhausted them both, but Saul didn't have anywhere else to look.

Fifty-five-year-old Molly, a widow, often says, "I just love my grandchildren. All four of them. If it weren't for them, I don't know who I'd be. My favorite things to do are to bake with them and take them to the movies." When they were little, she would have them come to her house, one at a time, for a special treat. At 13, her oldest grandchild revolted. He said he was too old to keep going to Grandma's house. He wanted to hang with his friends. And whose need was this staying overnight really meeting at this point? "Don't you understand, Grandma? I'm getting to be a man and that doesn't mix so well with a constantly doting grandmother." Molly hadn't done the work of finding other sources of self-esteem, especially within herself.

Debbie, age 65 and a longtime divorcee, finally retired from a long-term job with a long-term employer. She loved her kids and grandkids. She even loved her children's spouses. She loved her apartment and her friends. Somehow she knew, however, that she couldn't just stop working without doing something radical. She decided she wanted and needed to get deeply involved with a group of people who were making a difference in the world AND exploring who they were and could be in the process. Radical for Debbie turned out to be joining the Peace Corps and teaching in Southeast Asia. Her daughter had a fit. Her son said, "Good for you, Mom." Her sister said, "It's always been called Your Life for a reason. Whatever you choose, I will support you." Upon her return home after two years, Debbie found she still loved her children and her grandchildren and her apartment and her friends just as much as before but she didn't need them in the same way she used to. She had taken a risk and gotten to know herself—and new forms of self-esteem—by being a safe adventuress for a while.

KNOWLEDGE #6

How to have and keep the right professional advisors on your personal team.

Skill Set: The worst possible time to go looking for professional support is right after you have gone into a crisis situation. Can you predict EVERY professional need you may have for the rest of your life? Absolutely not. Something will happen that never occurred to you in advance. Still, is that a good reason to not have an established and ongoing relationship with all the advisors you predict you are going to need as you move into retirement, whatever form you choose, and further into your After 50 life? Look at your retirement and life ahead as you imagine it. Carefully record, review, and think about the asset exercise you did earlier in Chapter 4. Then think about the professionals you will need around you for everything from taxes to health. What do you need to be good at? Anticipate, talk with friends and colleagues to see who they respect among the specialty advisors, meet with the advisors, make choices, and start a relationship with the expectation that it will be long term.

Doug, age 67, had been having chest pains off and on for a long time. Either he didn't want to face it or he didn't believe he was vulnerable because admitting vulnerability about this meant admitting to a number of other vulnerabilities he didn't want to face either. As Ellen arrived home one evening from a meeting, Doug met her at the door with his hand clutched on his chest. "Don't take your coat off. I think you need to drive me to emergency. It's been much worse since this afternoon." They went straight to the emergency room. Who was Doug's primary care physician? He didn't have one. Who was his cardiologist? He didn't have one. Where were the medical history records that many wise people After 50 file with the hospital just in case they are needed? He hadn't done that.

KNOWLEDGE #7

How to skillfully develop a short-term plan, a mid-range plan, and long-term intention that make sense and can be adapted as necessary based on new or updated information.

Everyone, in my opinion, would do well to have an incremental three-segment retirement and life plan. The first segment, as we have discussed, is for the next 18 months. It's the most specific and focused because we stand a lot greater chance of being able to control or at least strongly influence what happens within the next 18 months than further out in time. The second section is the mid-term plan containing direction and steps, but not at the level of specifics that appear in section one. The third section is the longer-term plan, which often includes intentions and possible action steps but is the least-detailed and specific of the three sections.

Skill Set: Reviewing and updating your three-segment plan regularly, driven by a calendar cycle AND by responding to new information soon after it comes to you.

Phil, age 59, loved planning. Gloria, two years younger, almost always went along with his plans. He created a complete and concrete plan that ran like an unbroken ribbon from where he stood to way out in his future. He had it laid out month by month for the next 12 years. His plan included selling the house at the top of the market, renting an apartment for a while, retiring in two years, and buying a fifth-wheel trailer and a truck to travel around the U.S. for at least three years. That was his plan. What actually happened: Gloria became ill and now needs to be within a short distance of her substantial local medical resources, the market tanked and the sale of the house didn't make sense for the moment, his daughter got a divorce and moved in with Phil and Gloria "for a few months" until she got her feet firmly on the ground. Phil is now hatching an 18-month plan and putting off the rest of the longer-term plan until his dust settles.

KNOWLEDGE #8

How to be an After 50 life pioneer and live with the risk and impermanence that's a part of life today.

This doesn't mean disaster is lurking around every corner and it doesn't mean we need to avoid all risk. It doesn't mean being foolhardy, either. It does mean that our lives—and the world—are not as stable as they used to be and are slowly changing. This also doesn't mean that we shouldn't plan. Planning is a crucial part of getting to our futures as we imagine them. Plans must be shorter term in each of the three perspectives and also adaptable. We can have all the long-term intentions we want, but confusing them with a part of an ironclad plan that means we will have failed unless they come true is beyond baloney.

Great plans proceed to where we want to go but have significant tolerance for risk, impermanence, and surprises over time. Success is that the plan adapted and so did we, not that we executed on a rigid, long-term plan flawlessly.

Skill Set: Creating and maintaining a balance between our short-term goals and our long-term intentions. Certainly we need both, but the reality is that the former can be much more concrete, specific, and timelined than the latter.

Laura, age 56, and Rick, age 59, had short-term goals and long-term intentions. Their short-term goals included:

1. Being debt free
2. Building the cash reserves necessary to purchase a piece of property where they could build a house and raise dogs
3. Finding more time for each other

Their plan included a debt-elimination section complete with a budget, a savings plan also included in the overall budget, and a commitment that Sundays were for the two of them only. They would take turns planning nice Sundays. The great trap for both of them was getting ahead of themselves. They loved to go look at property and, almost always when they found one they liked, they suffered through the tight loop discussion of how to make a purchase work now without waiting. Then they both felt disappointed. Their long-term intention to purchase a piece of property remained and they didn't want to give up short-term window-shopping/looking. They agreed they needed an excellent, strategic step right after they went property hunting but before they went around the roller coaster again and become disappointed. They finally settled on going to see Laura's father, in whom they both adored and believed. The man was enormously practical and he was willing to do this for them whenever they felt the need. In the end, the short-term plan proceeded beautifully toward their financial goals. They needed some assistance to stay grounded in the short term without giving up property window-shopping. Laura's father was just the man they needed.

KNOWLEDGE #9

How to stay very healthy one day at a time.

Skill Set: These skills aren't magic. They are common sense that takes action behind them.

Seventy-four-year-old Denise was recovering from gall bladder surgery. She had a choice, according to her partner. She could either get a short-term health plan together or she could expect unending grief from Susan. Actually, how she felt after the surgery was the first thing in her entire life that made Denise feel really, unquestionably old.

She decided that at her age and in her condition, the only reasonable plan would be a repeatable, scalable short-term health plan. The plan components included:

1. Joining a health club that was actually a part of the extended hospital/medical center in their area.

2. Building a personal health network of four to five people in her own age group who could be exercise buddies with her, hear her workout commitments, and show up together. Denise knew it was all too easy to blow it off if she was doing it alone.
3. Buying an hour of a great nutritionist's time.
4. Walking to the local coffee hangout with Susan at least three times a week.
5. Minimizing alcohol intake.
6. Making an appointment with her doctor to ask, "What are the top five things you would like to ask me to do for my own good?"

What do you notice about these knowledge and skill sets? I notice that they are doable and require a combination of attention, discipline, patience, and adaptability. None of them will fit well inside a long-term, rigid plan. Like our lives, they must adapt to new realities—which doesn't mean always rolling over and accepting them. It does mean being strategic and smart about how and what to adapt.

Reader Exercise

1. Review each of the knowledge types above. On a scale of 1 to 10 (10 being great), rate how well you possess and use them in your life.
2. Given the answers, pick the two top types of knowledge you would like to improve and build a short-term (up to 18 months) plan to make that happen.
3. Show your answers and plan to someone you respect who is perceptive, candid, and not so close to you that their feedback will be diluted. If you don't have someone, ask one of your friends to recommend someone and open the connection door for you. Tell the person what he or she can do to support you and ask for the support.

Chapter 7

Sacrifices and Trade-offs

A s I've discussed, you are bound to encounter some sacrifices and trade-offs on your life straightaway, putting a curve or a twist where you hadn't thought one would be.

Dorian Mintzer, PhD, has over 40 years of experience as a therapist, life/retirement transition coach, money and relationship coach, consultant, writer, speaker, teacher, and group and workshop facilitator. She works with individuals and couples who are dealing with "what's next?" and want help to develop a sense of well-being as they navigate the "second half of life." (Dorian can be found at http://www.revolutionizeretirement.com.)

When I interviewed Dori, we spoke about how many transitions there are in an average life and how much we might have in common.

George: Do we really have that much in common?

Dorian: In a simplistic way, what we have in common is that all of us, if we're lucky, are going to get older and, in the process, experience multiple transitions, changes, and loses throughout our life. There are always "surprises" and "curveballs" that we have to deal with. What make each person unique, however, is how we handle and cope with these experiences. People vary in how they make sense of and frame the experience and how resilient or not they are. I'm often impressed with the variety of how differently people experience similar events. I believe that our response is partly influenced by how we've handled earlier transitions, changes, and loss and what we learned—or didn't learn—from those experiences.

If you're financially secure, they may only be small bumps in the road. However, regardless of financial status, these twists and curves around timing, family, professional, health, personal, or a combination of issues could be important to your future quality of life, retired or not.

This chapter will help you navigate through these encounters with soft and very hard choices, both of which can involve sacrifices and trade-offs.

What do I mean by sacrifice? I mean letting go, temporarily or permanently, of something you have held dear until now *but* that seems to be included in the price for achieving what you now think is most important in the short or long term.

Charlotte and Bill, both 71, had thought they would be fully retired by now. Bill did retire. Then he fell ill and, although the couple had medical insurance, their portion of the bills took nearly one-quarter of their retirement savings. Even after he recovered his health, Bill had extended periods of despondence. For quite a while he wasn't employable. This wasn't what he had planned when they created their long-term retirement plan. Charlotte sacrificed her own retirement expectations, continuing to work full-time as she had for years. They could easily live on her income as long as she had no health issues and a job, but they couldn't really replenish their retirement savings.

Elton and Laqueta, ages 56 and 54, had their children late in life. The four girls were 17, 16, 14, and 13. Elton had worked at the plant for 30 years on the day he learned the plant was being shut down permanently. Until that morning, retirement had been on the near horizon. The couple had talked about it often. Getting a good job at another plant would require the family to move to another state. A local competitor also offered him a job, which meant they wouldn't have to move, but at much less money. They had to evaluate their options. Should they move the girls to take the new job elsewhere or remain where they were but make far less money? In the end they decided to make the five-year sacrifice and stay where they were. Laqueta would go to work to make up some of the lost income. The girls, in what their parents saw as essential years, could stay in a stable, familiar, and supportive neighborhood and school environment. As the youngest approached age 18, the parents would take a hard look at what was best for just the two of them at that point and then make whatever changes were necessary.

What do I mean by trade-offs? I mean there are two or three things you want. You are going to have to choose between them because there isn't the money or time or energy for all of them at this juncture in life.

Maybe Danielle, age 68, and Matt, age 69, should have seen it coming, but they did not. They had worked together in the advertising business they had started, lived in their community for a long time, raised their kids and seen them off to their own lives, and been prominent in the business and social communities. They had grand retirement plans that included selling the business to one of their most senior employees. Unfortunately, in a recent economic downturn of epic proportions for their region, their clients stopped advertising. They didn't simply cut back but outright stopped. Even with some cash reserves, having no revenue was a huge problem when they also had a combination of a bank loan payment, monthly payments on the office building, payroll for the employees, and ongoing costs like insurance, website support, and the memberships and events in their town that made them prominent players. The couple wanted the business back on track and themselves back on the retirement track. Danielle and Matt were deeply attached to being business owners, partners, and in charge. The financial solution that presented itself was an investment in their company by a large statewide firm. They would no longer have majority, much less total ownership. On the other hand, the business would have the resources to survive almost indefinitely and the two could continue to work their way back to prosperity and their retirement. They were face-to-face with the biggest trade-off of their working lives: Sell a majority interest in the business to give it a secure future or remain in full control of their much less secure organization.

We could devote significant attention here to anticipating all possible types of situational, expected, and unexpected sacrifices and trade-offs. I'd rather not do that because I think you already get it. What I would like to do, however, is provide you with an alternative approach to help you manage these trade-offs. That's what the rest of Chapter 7 is all about.

A TEMPLATE TO ASSIST WITH DECISIONS, SACRIFICES, AND TRADE-OFFS

Sacrifices and trade-offs may be an essential part of crafting your future together with inspiration and opportunity as you go along. If the answers to high-quality questions don't include the possibility of at least short-term sacrifices and trade-offs, there could be something wrong with your questions and answers or both.

"There" (as in Finally Got There to stay and don't have to face any of this ever again) may need to be one of the sacrifices. And trade-offs are already an essential part of many smart, informed decision-making processes.

Remember our earlier conversation and work about how the quality of the question drives the quality of the answer? It's true, and we're going to work with that concept again.

Here is my own current template. It doesn't change very much or very often. Not that it can't change, but I've been doing this for so long the winnowing process is settled, at least for now. You don't need to know exactly what I mean by each characteristic word to get the picture. Doing this leads us to use our perspective abilities and see the big picture about ourselves and our lives. Remember that the characteristic words in the left column are my own, for example purposes, and should be replaced by your own.

You've already begun answering the questions—and are on the way to completing the template—if you really did the work in each of the preceding chapters. Figure 7-1 is my template for my purposes and choices in my life.

Figure 7-1. George's template.

The qualities I would most like to have characterize my future life.	How true are they now in my life?	What specifically has to change, including sacrifices and trade-offs?	How will I make that happen? And when?
Clean (transactions with myself and others)			
Creative			
Harmonious			
Abundant			
Free			
Healthy			
Responsible			
Interested and Interesting (my form of curious)			

Reader Exercise

Here is your own blank template (see Figure 7-2). The information we are seeking, for now, is limited to the left column only.

Stop and take some time to decide what qualities you would truly like to characterize your near-term future life. If you need to discuss with someone else, please do so BUT remember that in the end, the characteristics need to be of your selection, not the other person's.

As I mentioned in the last chapter, you should find someone who is perceptive and candid and will provide honest feedback to you. Take your time. It has to get done, but this is not a power exercise in which success is beating the clock or leaving no spaces unfilled. This is your life we're talking about. It's important to me . . . and to you.

I had to make a decision here. Was I going to give you the whole template at this point OR was I going to only show you the left column? The upside of only showing you the left column is that I don't run the risk of losing your attention or having you get way ahead of where we are in this exercise. The downside of only showing you the left column is that your characteristic qualities are disembodied from the emergence of the short-, mid-, and long-term pieces of your retirement and life plan.

I've chosen to give you the complete template and ask you to work on the left column only. After that's done and you are satisfied with its contents for now, please feel free to work on the rest of the template.

Figure 7-2. Your turn.

What are the qualities I would most like to have characterize my life over the next 18 months?	How true are they of my life now?	What specifically has to change, including sacrifices and trade-offs?	How will I make that happen? And when?

At this point in the book and our process, you should begin to see your retirement or life plan—all three perspectives—begin to come together in your head.

While we're at it, knowing that you will shortly be moving across the template and your plan will begin to emerge, let's revisit some of the most important information and high-quality questions we covered earlier in the book.

- What in your life that you are good at now will serve you well in the future? What will not? Samantha has been instrumental all through her husband's medical career and medical practice build. Her skill at drawing new medical talent into her husband's professional community is legendary. All of their community friends are beginning to retire and move away. Her husband is talking about it also and doesn't expect to replenish his local contacts. How will these skills help her in the future? How could they get in her way?
- What roles that you now occupy will serve you well in the future? Which will not? Which have already come to an end but you are pretending they have not? Lynn is a professional woman and a really involved, dominant mother. She and her husband have one daughter, now age 24, who is just getting around to moving out of her parents' home. The daughter never made the connection between her major and future work satisfaction/employability until after she graduated. Lynn is now 55. How long will the dominant role of mother continue to serve Lynn and her daughter well? When could it begin to get in her way and how?
- Who in your life now will serve you well and vice versa in the future? Who will not? Which of these relationships represents a larger network of connections that will need to be nurtured or eliminated? Terry is still working more than full-time and loves it. He has lots of friends, so many he can hardly keep up with all of them. His best friend has announced his retirement and rededication of his life to improving his golf score. Also a lawyer, he hopes that he can leave all talk of law behind in retirement. The two men had a lot in common until now,

but their life roadways are beginning to diverge rapidly. How valuable is this relationship likely to be to Terry in the future?

- Which physical objects are you hanging on to from habit and a reluctance to let go? Which physical objects will fit into your future and serve you well? The same goes for relationships. Which will be most useful to you in the future?

- When she was a girl in the 1940s and 1950s, George's mother collected demitasse cups. When she died, George inherited the collection. They have been packed away for many years. George is sentimental about the cups. He doesn't have a place to display them. His children and grandchildren don't want them. He feels as if he would be throwing away his mother's girlhood by disposing of them. How well are these demitasse cups likely to serve George in the future?

It's time to take a kind of inventory. As we progress through our lives, many of us have a decreasing capacity to haul an excessive number of physical tokens and history around with us.

There is a huge danger here that we will leap into action, abandoning and tossing aside without reflection or common sense. Excessive action here looks like no criteria, little thought, and a kind of temporary obsession.

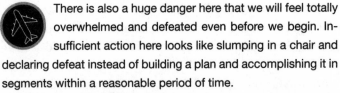 There is also a huge danger here that we will feel totally overwhelmed and defeated even before we begin. Insufficient action here looks like slumping in a chair and declaring defeat instead of building a plan and accomplishing it in segments within a reasonable period of time.

Like in the story of "Goldilocks and the Three Bears," it needs to be not too action filled and not too unplanned. It needs to be just right. And the balance of action filled and planned will probably ebb and flow over time. This is sometimes known as balance and harmony.

BACK TO SACRIFICES AND TRADE-OFFS

I don't want to move on without making some recommendations about sacrifices and trade-offs for your consideration.

Sometimes we will see them coming. Sometimes we won't. They may be something we chose. They could also be something that is imposed on us. Whichever combination you face at any given moment, comparing them to your template of characteristics should help inform your sacrifice or trade-off choices.

It's easy, and even natural, for us to focus on what's going on in the moment—be it a problem of your own or a loved one's, an opportunity, a sudden curve in the roadway of life, or getting what you've wanted and not quite knowing what to do with it—and deal with it as a one-off situation and move on. Even if we make great one-off decisions in the heat of the moment and take excellent one-off actions, they are unlikely to come together in a coherent way when we look back at them over our shoulder and wonder how we got to where we are. We each need the larger framework of intended life characteristics within which to make smart decisions/take actions that are congruent and really helpful in the long run.

When I am working with career clients, I frequently have to remind them that a series of jobs, even good jobs, do not make a career. They are just a series of employment situations. To make a career, you need a series of jobs that link together to build 1) an evolving combination of marketable experience and expertise, 2) an increasing opportunity for future promotion and/or income increase, 3) the network of relationships that are helpful now and will be even more helpful in the future, and 4) a way to stay even with or ahead of the curve for what employers and industries are going to need in the future. This kind of career management is not only applicable to jobs. This is also applicable to that cluster of work for pay we know variously as freelancing, project work, the gig economy, entrepreneurial activities, and self-employment. Great career management requires longer-term intentions, an incremental plan, and regular updating based on new information.

The same applies to our retirement and life planning. Current decisions and activities made with an eye to one's thoughtful and periodically updated/overarching list of desired life characteristics are much more likely to have a positive, rolling effect on overall life satisfaction and success than those that happen on a strictly one-off, heat-of-the-moment basis.

You are going to be sailing through uncharted waters. Your compass won't work because magnetic forces keep changing. If you have a North Star, a set of guiding characteristics for your future, you can know you are generally going in the right direction.

SACRIFICES TO CONSIDER MAKING

Roles in Which You Are Solidified Like Fruit in Jell-O

You can see out but you can't move much. By the time we are 50 or older, many of us are almost inseparable from our roles and the doing that comes with them. It's how we know who we are, what contributions we are making, what we like and don't like, and what we are growing tired of. All of us have multiple roles. It's how other people know us best—beyond our names and faces—and it's frequently how they think of us whether they know it or not. Sometimes it's healthier not to immediately replace a role that we are leaving or is leaving us, letting some time go by and some dust settle before deciding when and if to replace it.

Brian is a banker. He goes to the bank every morning and comes home every night. He has for years. He sells banking services as easily as he breathes. He actually has a bathrobe with the bank's crest on it. His community activities—and the awards he has been given because of them—have all been oriented around the bank. His role as visible community banker has probably been even more important than the next two on his priority list, husband and father. In a year and a half, Brian is going to retire. How well will this role serve him after retirement AND is there anything he should be doing to prepare for change before he actually retires?

Totally and Permanently There/Completion

Most people love the sense of recognition and reward with having arrived at completion. We're finally there. We ran the course and finished well. We NEVER, EVER have to worry about or do that again. Whoops. Hold it a minute. It's great to celebrate milestones and achievements. We are naturally doers and achievers and problem solvers. It's in our culture. We graduate from college or get married or choose a career path with an amazing (and frequently self-deceiving) sense of permanence. Where "there" and "completion" get us into trouble is if they come with the assumption that we'll never have to face this again or something is totally behind us. We're past it. Whew! Only this probably doesn't occur as often as we would like.

Brenda had a terrible time finding the right boyfriend. In the end, she couldn't get along with them. So she focused on her career without much regret except for the difficulty she had in getting along with some of her male colleagues. Later in life—in her 50s—a fellow proposed and she said yes. Her assumption was that, once married, she had arrived; she was there; she would never have to deal with it again. No one told her that marriage is a work in progress, not a permanent arrangement at which you have arrived. Brenda and her husband are seeing a marriage counselor. She didn't understand how fluid and spontaneous marriage can be.

The Do Trap

A friend of 35 years just sent me a text message. She was "blubbering" at the top of a ladder from frustration. In her mid-60s she is one of the most independent, determined, and driven people I know. And that's saying something. Her email concluded with the notion that no matter how hard she has tried otherwise, in her heart she still believes she is only as good as what she can get done today. She feels she has no permanent value. There she is at the top of the ladder high up in her garage only to discover she needed another set of hands and couldn't do it by herself. Does she need to stop doing? Probably not. Will she be able to do less as she grows older? Probably. What needs to change? Her utter dependence upon her daily doing for her personal sense of value, place, and worth. There is nothing wrong with doing. The difficulty—the trap—is if you have no sense of yourself and instead have diminished worth if you aren't doing.

Relationships That Don't Serve Us
Well Anymore

Ryan and Jennifer were friends with the couple who lived next door for years. They had boys and girls the same ages. The kids were inseparable. Almost everything was about the kids in those years: scouts, school, sports, dance lessons, piano recitals, giggling kids underfoot and always running in and out. They were extended family for each other and always there to back each other up. Only when the last of the kids graduated from high school did it occur to the parents how little they actually had in common as adults. For a long time, they tried going out to dinner periodically but always ended up talking about where the kids were and what they were up to. The neighbors continued to love those conversations. Ryan and Jennifer eventually became bored to death. They were still parents, of course, but through the passing years they had each developed other interests, friends, and possibilities. The dinners, painfully, grew further and further apart until they stopped entirely.

Objects, Including Our History
and Others' History

"Are you finally ready to get rid of your childhood tennis racket and that swimming trophy from your fifth-grade swim team?" Alice asked her husband, Phil. "We've dragged that stuff through four houses now."

"That set of glasses belongs to my parents. They were wedding presents," Phil exclaimed. "And how about those tablecloths taking up so much room in the drawer? They belonged to your mother but you never want to use them because they are so much work to wash and then perfectly iron." Alice put her hands on her hips. "Unfortunately, I'm getting less and less romantic about your parents' glasses and my parents' tablecloths. When we were first married, they were historic treasures, proof of our being grown-ups ourselves, and a connection to our own family stories. All four of our parents have been gone a long time now. I'm for getting rid of all of them, but let's sit down first and ask the smartest questions we can. One, what of all this stuff is really important to us other than the last connections to our parents? Two, what benefit is any of this stuff to us now and in the future? Three, is there anything here any of the kids would like and we won't feel like we're dumping stuff on them? If we can agree there is no benefit and we can each keep two objects that connect us to our parents, let's agree we're putting our After 50 skills to good use and move ahead."

Excessively Secure, Familiar, and Comfortable

"What's the point of planning if this author keeps saying we can only have a five-year horizon? Sounds like a lot of work to me to create a plan, update it constantly, adapt the plan and ourselves to the emerging realities, and then do it all over again. I know change is happening. Nevertheless, I don't see it affecting us very much. I just want a 15-year plan that will come true. I want us to create it, type it into the computer, print it out to prove we did it, put in a file, and revisit every five years to celebrate how on track we continue to be. Otherwise it's just work and who needs that?" It's easy to trick ourselves into thinking that a plan is the same as a guarantee. It's also easy for many of us to assume that if things don't go according to plan we're somehow being punished like children. The fact is, plans are an important set of intentions. They aren't guarantees.

A Sense of Having Decided on
Our Irrefutable Favorites

"I like my meat and potatoes. They are a metaphor for me of comfort, familiarity, and stability. When I was a kid, China might as well have been on another planet. Italy was where other kids' grandparents or great grandparents came from. Syria, who had ever heard of Syria? And Africa was a far-off land populated by wild beasts and head hunters. I like my meat and potatoes. Why do you need to keep exposing me to other cuisines and strange flavors? I'm standing here saying I like my meat and potatoes and you want me to go out for Ethiopian food tonight? Have you no mercy or shame?" No doubt, we are entitled to having our favorites. However, it's dangerously easy to settle into having the same favorites at 58 that we had at 18. They are comfortable, familiar, and untroubling. It's also dangerously tempting to blame others—using shame—to avoid trying new things. When is your favorite really a favorite? When is your favorite actually the product of untested and unchallenged repetition? Only you can know.

Goal Addiction

"We all benefit from having goals, dear. But as we get older, if we're only as good as our most recent accomplishment, we have failed to get off the merry-go-round of our 30s and 40s. What can I say of the 70-year-old who sincerely believes he is only as good as his golf score this morning or his last card game winnings? What can I say of a man, my husband, who absolutely cannot rest until he has killed both an alligator and a lion with a bow and arrow? I'm happy you have goals. They should, however, be an integrated part of supporting what we want our life to be for the next 10 years. I feel like you leave the 'what we want our life to be like' part up to me while you move your ego from proof to proof and goal to goal, utterly unrelated to your participation in the quality of our life together. I'm getting really tired of it."

For many of us, goals have been a way of life. Losing weight. Making money. Taking better care of ourselves and our loved ones. Visiting every continent. Owning a house. Getting an MBA or an MA. Getting the kids into a great college. They gave us energy. Saving enough money—a nickel or dime or quarter at a time—to buy a new bicycle. Goals gave us excitement and purpose. They validated and caressed us with the pleasure of achievement. We moved from goal to goal. Do we continue to need goals After 50? Absolutely, yes. Then what's so different about the role of goals After—and well After—50?

MY STORY

When I was a little boy, cake was all about the frosting. The baked part existed as a foundation for the greater, more important, exterior sweetness. My father always wanted a cherry or rhubarb pie for his birthdays. I thought he was absolutely nuts. Neither of us understood the cake metaphor at the time.

Through the years, I have come to appreciate the fullness of the cake and frosting together. I no longer eat the cake part first to get it out of the way for the real main event: the frosting.

Cake and frosting are a metaphor to me now. I still want the frosting and get pleasure from it. Yet, over time, the focus and combination has subtly shifted. I am more like the cake, substantial and freestanding and solid. The goal achievement is now more like the frosting: important, stimulating, colorful, and sweet. I still get a lot from it and often want more, but—like the cake—I'm solid and OK regardless of the frosting. Frosting decorates the core or cake. It isn't the core.

This is what I would wish for all of us as we plan and live our retirement and our lives: lots of sweetness and the right kinds of goal/achievement stimulation for a high-quality retirement and life. But we no longer have to be dependent upon it—either its size or recentness—for us to be deeply OK. Instead we are our own favorite, well-blended, solid kind of cake that benefits from frosting but no longer needs it as evidence or proof or source of primary, temporary identity.

If you aren't OK unless you have a recent goal achievement and at least one in process, then you might want to reconsider goals and whether or not you have a goal addiction. I totally believe in goals and achievement over 50, but not as the primary, and in some cases only, way to be OK.

TRADE-OFFS TO CONSIDER MAKING

A Smart Amount of Risk

"I understand your need to be careful, dear. We have money but not to burn. Here we are in our 50s. I'm focusing on what we want our life to be like while you are focusing on taking as few risks as possible to conserve and protect what we have. I think we have recuperative years now that we won't have in our 70s if something goes wrong. We have time to plan. We have time to start small with little capital and low overhead. I really want to start this small, weekend business now as part of our retirement plan. Only living on savings might be a dumb idea 25 years from now. What would happen if we had a small, reliable income stream in addition AND equity in a small business that we could eventually sell. I'm asking you to take the right amount of smart risk with me now as an investment in our future."

Short-Term Planning

Short-term planning is an ongoing, living, breathing process. It becomes long-term planning through updating and adapting iteratively over time. Well done, short-term planning is combined with the right amount of effort in a cycle that repeatedly includes research and conclusion. See the Learning and Decision Making Loop (Figure 3-1).

Replenished Networks of Colleagues and Friends and Skill/Expertise-Based Connections

In this highly connected, expanding world, it's seldom possible for us to know all the people and have all of the necessary expertise. We're going to live longer and work longer. We're going to need more money to pay for those years. We're going to have to have new and upgraded skills—not to mention vitality—to find our places in the radically altering world of work for pay, which may eventually look at least as much like freelancing as it has looked like permanent jobs in the past. This all means we need access to the people who are known by the people we know/are connected to. This means understanding and effectively using all the technological tools necessary for an expanded, effective professional footprint in the world of work for pay. This means—and we are finite beings—focusing for the most part on those professional relationships that can make the difference and open doors for us.

Empty Space Technique

I like using what I call the empty space. You can design your own. Mine looks like a large room with hardwood floors and high, hardwood ceiling, glass walls with drapes that can be closed at night, comfortable ambient lighting, a gas stove that looks like a kiva, and a front door. That's it. No rugs or furniture. When I remove something from my life—an object or a role or a skill or something that gave me comfort and I depended upon in the past but no longer will serve me well—my trade-off is that I can, however briefly, grieve its passing by spending some time in my quiet, empty space. My discipline is that I cannot rush out and find anything at all to fill the recently emptied space. First, I have to make friends, yet again, with the empty space and settle into its comfort. Then I go through the Learning and Decision Making Loop (see Chapter 3) to observe and choose what I want, if anything, to take up the space recently occupied and now not. Usually I end up comfortable with the empty space and without desire to put anything in it. Sometimes I simply announce silently to the world that I have some empty space and am awaiting the unplanned arrival of the unplanned thing that will be perfect for the space. Occasionally, I remember that I've always wanted X (object, role, etc.) and previously didn't have life space for it. So I go and check it out to see if I still really want it and if it will fit into the space available without massive rearranging of everything else.

A Different Kind of Deciding and Learning

Most of us came out of a learning culture, which assumed what we didn't know. An expert (content and teaching) organized the information, we learned (memorized it through rote or physical repetition), and we aspired to get an A on the quiz or at least to pass it so we could move on to the next one. Most of us also saw learning as something to accomplish and move beyond to the next item on our calendar or agenda. In fact, it doesn't work that way when creating intentions, having a plan, updating the plan periodically, and updating ourselves and our perspectives as well. It doesn't end and we can't move beyond it. We can ignore it, but that works against us in the short and long term.

A different starting point for learning is going to be frequently required of us between 50 and elderly. We may or may not like it but it will be required anyway. The new starting point won't be acknowledging what we don't know and pursuing the necessary learning. It will be a variation of "I Don't Know What I Don't Know." It's called pioneering for a reason. There will be no one with greater expertise regarding your life than you have. There will be experts with recommendations, but the choices to be made will all be yours. Imagine you step, like a pilgrim, off a ship onto a beach with a big rock. You don't know the territory. You don't know the culture. You don't know the topography. You don't know the rules. What you already know could be wonderful or useless. You don't know how much of either one. Welcome to I Don't Know What I Don't Know. It's the starting place for all pioneers. The new learning process will look like our Chapter 3 Learning and Decision Making Loop viewed from its side, like a bedspring or an ascending coil. Every rotation takes us from I Don't Know What I Don't Know to I Know What I Don't Know, to finding the necessary resources and experience so we can learn it, to knowing it and then coming face-to-face, as learning loops will tend to do, with the next instance of I Don't Know What I Don't Know. This will apply in work for pay, health, updating social networks, financial decision making, and lots of other life arenas.

By the time we are 50 years old, we will have to renew our conscious effort to replenish our educations and marketable skill sets, our key relationships, and our attitude toward change and the world. It won't be just a matter of taking some classes and memorizing the material. We may well have to think and socialize in ways that are brand new to us. Here, moving rapidly into action— to reduce our anxiety or check an action off the list or spare us from facing what's really going on—will work against us. Certainly we'll need action but only in balance with the other stops on the learning loop.

Once again, this requires paying attention and working with what is, rather than working with what we wish. A rich and rewarding life requires conscious health of all kinds, including learning and adaptability health. I realize we have covered much more material than sacrifices and trade-offs. In addition to looking at them, we have seized the opportunity to build the bigger life context—what you are choosing to characterize your future—and built a tool that can and should be updated and revisited regularly.

And we've pulled a number of pieces together so that your three-perspective retirement or life plan is beginning to emerge.

Now on to Handling the Surprises and the Curves.

chapter 8

Handling the Surprises and Curves

Okay. Where are we now? Your three-perspective plan is beginning to emerge. Your intentions are more focused and you can clearly see the importance of paying attention, being adaptable, and having a plan that is built in segments from fairly concrete in the immediate future to a set of intentions and ideas extending out toward the further time horizon.

SURPRISES AND CURVES HAPPEN

I am suggesting that only a minority of us end up with surprises that demand a whole new plan from scratch because so much Continuous and Discontinuous Change has happened that the cleanest and surest way through is to start over. I am also suggesting, however, that very, very few of us will craft a plan at age 50 or later that won't change and that we can execute flawlessly for the rest of our lives, which could be a very long time for those of us who prove to have extreme longevity. Life, surprises, and changes of mind are more than likely to intervene somehow.

Surprises can, of course, come in an entire array of forms. Some give us well-advanced warning. Many do not. Some are within our control. Many are not.

We're cruising along a straightaway and, boom, suddenly there is a curve. Or a series of adjacent curves we didn't see that we were approaching.

What forms can they take? They can include, but aren't limited to:

- Our own or others' health.
- Financial condition changes.
- Work and employment changes.
- Interruption or termination of leisure because of necessity or lack of interest; the sudden irrelevance of roles long depended upon for our identity and self-esteem.
- Major change(s) in our social networks, especially our immediate and familiar network of the people we trust the most.
- Something someone else does that we think reflects badly on us and we don't want to be associated with it anymore. Here are several examples: Example #1: Your business partner does something that you think is borderline unethical. Example #2: The team captain of your baseball team strikes someone on the opposing team in a fit of bad temper. Example #3: A fellow member of a nonprofit board consciously and publicly misrepresents something you really believe in.
- Residential and community changes.
- An unanticipated change in our interests and passions.
- The return to our nest of children and grandchildren.
- The arrival in our nest of needy elders whether from our own family or someone else's.

Sixty-six-year-old Betty was enjoying her first year of retirement. She could see that down the road she might want and need to add more structure or activity to her life, but she didn't want that right now. She knew she wouldn't have to be a caregiver for elders because both of her parents were deceased. One day her closest cousin called to say that she had a big problem. Her cousin was going to have to accept a work transfer three states away or lose her job. The kicker was that, at least in the beginning, she couldn't take her elderly mother, Betty's favorite aunt, with her because she had no idea where or how she would live yet. Could her mother come to live with Betty for a while? Aunt Jane, now 87, had always been especially kind to Betty, doing all those special little things that parents often don't have time to do but grandparents and aunts and uncles may do regularly. Aunt Jane was still intellectually crisp but physically frail. She needed support but neither Betty nor her cousin could imagine putting Jane in a care facility at this point. What was Betty to do? Of course, she said, "Yes."

"But this wasn't in my plan! This can't be happening to me! Why me or us? Why now?" said Betty.

These are statements and questions based on weak evidence, the irrational idea that, if we didn't anticipate it, it shouldn't be happening. While it makes sense emotionally for a few minutes or hours, if it's extended it makes moving forward to adapt and alter our plans even more difficult than the driving circumstances themselves.

"Darn. I hate being surprised. I know I can't see everything coming or build a plan that covers absolutely all contingencies forever, but it still stings. Having said that, I guess it's time to adapt again, both my plan and myself. What does this surprise mean for me/us and our plan? What has to adapt, how fast, and for how long? How will I have to change my thinking and priorities?" This kind of reaction accelerates moving forward to a new, well-thought-out situation and ways to deal with it.

My job here is to talk about some ways to approach surprises and curves. It will help to see more clearly what is happening from more than one viewpoint. That will give you more informed perspectives and alternative ways to think about your experiences as they happen and afterward.

It's an uninformed and inaccurate assumption to think about the period between age 50 and elderly as one single period. It's as naïve as assuming all Baby Boomers are alike, needing and wanting the same things at the same time. It is naïve because it sets us up to be surprised and less adaptable when change—voluntary and involuntary—arrives.

I also think the period between age 50 and elderly is best described as three overlapping periods, not defined by age. They are defined by life situation, and different people arrive at them at different ages and from different circumstances.

A FEW WORDS ABOUT STAGE THEORY

Stage Theories attempt to organize and cluster different experiences or periods of our lives or the processes we go through. I admire Stage Theories as a way to understand and organize our experiences but not as a rigid and mandatory and highly validated road map of how we all must operate.

One example of a Stage Theory is Elizabeth Kübler-Ross's Five Stages of Grief: denial, anger, bargaining, depression, and acceptance. One goes through grief by going through these stages in order until emerging at the other end. I think this is a brilliant way to understand grief and how we deal with it. I don't think life is as tidy as progressing through 1, 2, 3, 4, and 5, like a row of hurdles, to the end of the race. Instead, I think it's much messier than that. While the stages, in their order, may be representative, in practice I think we tend to ricochet and wobble and loop around our progress forward in very individual ways that make our path look much more like a wavy line than a straight roadway. A client once said, "I must be doing something wrong about my grief. I'm finally feeling fairly accepting, which would be great if it weren't for my suspicion that I haven't done this right because I wasn't depressed long enough."

Why do I think keeping Stage Theory in mind will help with surprises and curves? Because in taking a good look at yourself in the midst of change you can see that, regardless of how permanent it seems in the moment, in fact, the developmental opportunity is to move through it to something as good or even better. This information is important to keep in mind because I'm going to introduce what I think of as a non-stage Period Theory. You'll see and I'll explain when we get there.

A FEW WORDS ABOUT DISTINGUISHING BETWEEN "IT'S PAINFUL BUT I'M RIGHT ON SCHEDULE" AND "SOMETHING IS DEFINITELY WRONG WITH ME THAT NEEDS FIXING"

Early on in this book, I made an important distinction between therapy based on the medical model (diagnosis, treatment, and cure) versus a developmental psychology approach that tends to assume there is nothing wrong with you that needs a cure (i.e., there is nothing wrong with you if you are bored after doing the same job for 10 years). What you are experiencing in your life may be painful but is right on schedule (the kids are going away and being an empty nester sounds more wonderful in theory than it is turning out to be in practice), or a developmental opportunity may be lurking as a large gift as a result of what is happening now (your friends have pushed you into dating, something you have been afraid of after years as a divorced person) and you are actually having a good time and discovering aspects of yourself you had forgotten.

Why is this information important to working with surprises and curves? If you go back to our work on assessing where you are and identifying your assets, a significant asset was your professional advisors. You don't necessarily have to have two psychological advisors: one for therapy and one for developmental purposes. Lots of great professionals out there do both. What you do need, in my opinion, is to understand which situation you think you are in and which approach you are looking for because that's what will help you make great choices about whom to work with and what to focus on.

You have come to a surprise or a curve. You will have to adapt. Your plan will have to adapt. Maybe the surprise or curve really represents a more dramatic instance of Continuous Change. Maybe the surprise or curve represents a game-changing, totally discontinuous situation or opportunity. Either way, you will need to think about which kind of change has arrived at your doorstep and whether or not it indicates something is wrong with you that needs fixing OR if it's painful but nothing is wrong with you and this is a developmental moment and opportunity that's more about clarity and adapting than it is about diagnosis, treatment, and cure.

THE IMPORTANCE OF TAKING THINGS
IN MANAGEABLE BITES

Earlier in this book we dealt with the importance of having three perspectives: up close/short term, mid-range, and far away/long term. This is crucial not only because it immediately brings your short-term priorities into full view, it also reduces the stress load because you can work with the shorter term first before you move out into the more distant and relative future.

The same technique applies to handling the surprises and the curves by taking them in perspective bites. Sometimes you will experience Continuous Change, which you may or may not see coming. Regardless, it's unlikely to be a total game changer, the equivalent of a bomb going off in the pattern and assumptions of your life. Sometimes you will experience Discontinuous Change and, by definition, you are unlikely to see it coming. On top of that it may momentarily confuse you into thinking there is something wrong with you. Probably not. You will be suddenly faced with having to rapidly see the size, robustness, and implications of something you haven't experienced before that's a game changer.

In order to minimize the surprises and curves of your upcoming years, I'd like to propose that, based on years of observations and working with clients, there is a kind of ebb and flow that happens. I offer this to you, not as a locked-in Stage Theory in which you must do all the work of one stage before advancing to the next climbing through a row of box cars in motion behind a locomotive. I offer this to you as a way to see in advance some of the surprises and curves that so many others have experienced.

A Non-Stage Period Theory as a Window onto Surprises and Curves

I especially like this way of understanding our lives because it doesn't come with the prejudices and assumptions of homogenous, age-driven, inflexible models. And it assumes that our priorities and plans are inevitably going to change to reflect what we don't want/can't have anymore and what we've discovered we would like that we hadn't needed to focus on until now.

New Freedom

The first of these periods, which I call New Freedom, often begins with becoming empty nesters around age 50, totally unaccustomed to the new discretionary space, income, time, and possibilities. Remember, it's an individual experience, so age is not an absolute predictor of this period in our lives. It also includes people whose career ambitions are significantly met so that their relationship to work and ambition has been modified. They stop being consumed by their work like a man who looks up and suddenly realizes—to his surprise—that different priorities are emerging. The reverse is also true. Someone who has stayed at home for decades when suddenly faced with freedom may want to consider exploring options. Discretionary life space is suddenly available. Priorities shift. It can take some getting used to. People in this period often find themselves at least temporarily disoriented by having or taking additional time, space, and planning after years of incessant commotion and action. It is kind of like pushing on a rock for years and it suddenly moves, changing all assumptions.

Sam's New Freedom Story

Sam went to law school, the first in his family to graduate from college, much less graduate from a prominent law school. He chose family law, especially divorces, as his specialty early on because it would allow him to make a lot of money and work with individuals to solve and move beyond complex emotions and problems.

At age 25 he began to practice law, got married, and began to raise a family. On his 33rd birthday he announced to his wife and children that he would spend 17 more years as a divorce attorney and that on his 50th birthday he would quit and then do something else. He repeated this statement to his family on each of his next 16 birthdays. "Sure, sure, Dad!" his family said each year.

While he liked practicing law, Sam was clear with himself all along that it wouldn't be his life's work until he keeled over. He wanted at least a second career if not, eventually, a third. At noon on his 50th birthday he came home, something so unusual that his wife wanted to know what he was doing there. "I've been telling you for years that on my 50th birthday I'd stop practicing law. That's today. Here I am."

"But what will you do?" asked his startled wife. "I'm going to be supportive but I don't want you at home every day getting underfoot and suddenly supervising me." "I haven't had much time to think about it until today," he replied, "but I think I'll spend the next six months working with someone who specializes in midlife career change. In fact, I think you should join me because you are about to have an involuntary career change. The kids are going to go away within two years and you will be para-unemployed."

They sat down at the table in the kitchen with a sandwich and coffee, beginning to work with the fact that they both were happily entering a period of New Freedom but having only a hazy idea of what to do about it.

Masie and Clifton's New Freedom Story

Masie and Clifton, ages 59 and 67, had been married and in business together for years. They owned a landscaping business, selling specialized gardens—installation and maintenance—to real estate developers, golf courses, residential builders, parks departments, and other customers. They had worked hard, made sure their company was always positioned as a woman-owned company (Masie was always the face of the business; Clifton primarily worked with the sod growers), raised a family, and now, in their mid-50s, were making plans to sell the business.

Their son, Jezel, graduated from college and returned home with a shocking announcement. Having looked at all of his employment options, he wanted to join his parents in their business and eventually buy them out.

Masie and Clifton had always assumed they would retire upon selling the business, not anticipating an interest by any of their children who had all claimed they could hardly wait to get out and explore the world professionally. Still, they were pleased and proud that Jezel had discovered a real interest in owning a business, and theirs in particular.

They worked out a 10-year buyout with their son. His stipulation was that both of his parents remain working in the business for at least five years. They could come and go as they wanted provided they worked enough to keep everything on an even keel while Jezel worked full-time.

Suddenly, instead of having full-time freedom, they had part-time New Freedom. For Masie and Clifton, it turned out to be a real blessing. They didn't have to go instantly from full-time work to no work. They could have some time to explore their options and get used to having space, time, and freedom—at least part-time. And they had the satisfaction of knowing that the business they had worked so hard to create would have an extended life. They were free in just the right amount for the transition period.

Jackie's New Freedom Story

Jackie, age 68, had worked for a major national bank for years. She had risen from teller in the early years to branch manager in her mid-career to regional manager later in her career. She had a reputation for being really smart, beautifully dressed at all times, and always cordial if a bit distant. For a variety of reasons, Jackie had never married, devoting herself instead primarily to her work and to her small army of nieces and nephews who adored her.

What most people didn't know about Jackie was she had an artistic side. She loved clothes, especially shoes, and spent much of her leisure time sketching new designs for everything from shoes to earrings. During her vacations, she had sometimes attended sessions at a New York design school.

Five years before her retirement, Jackie crafted a plan for herself. She developed an online design business with one employee—herself. She marketed her services and began to supply apparel designs to clothing manufacturers. This was an evenings- and weekends-only effort for the most part. Now, as she approaches her retirement and with a small but successful apparel design business, she is looking forward to New Freedom. Maybe she will grow her business. Maybe she will sell it. Maybe . . . ? She is intent on living with the New Freedom after retirement. Then she can decide what's next.

New Horizons

The second of these periods, which I call New Horizons, usually begins after New Freedom has been around for a while and we're comfortable with having some open, uncommitted life space. New Horizons involves greater focus and clarity about where we want to take the freedom, what we're curious about, how we want to spend our energy, and how we're going to move into being good at this new phase of life. A year after the last of her kids left for college, Alice took a job. She wanted the experience of still being a breadwinner and more routine/structure to her days. None of her friends saw that coming.

Six months after finally making VP in his company, Peter suddenly took up wheel-turned pottery. He had to work even harder as a VP than he had at any other time in his career BUT he was no longer willing to be consumed by it. Peter knew he had the freedom to make choices. He wanted something he could pick up and put down that was both creative and demanding away from work. None of his colleagues saw this coming.

Joanna and Dennis Cole's New Horizons Story

Joanna and Dennis Cole, both 59, have been empty nesters for a while. They have enjoyed their New Freedom and they took advantage of the time to explore at length what they want and don't want in their individual lives and their life together.

Self-employed, to his surprise Dennis wants to retire and is planning to do so in two years. He will sell his dental practice to his younger associate and is negotiating the sale now. He is surprised how much he is looking forward to no longer being responsible for a business yet continuing to work part-time, tapping into his creative side. Always into fine metal work with his hands, Dennis decided he would like to be a jewelry maker and sculptor, traveling to fine craft fairs and making custom pieces for clients.

Once that piece of his life was clear to Dennis, he invested in some home equipment and materials. He also began taking fine arts classes at their local university and museum. While he doesn't know what he will do with all of his time, he knows what will make him happy with a significant portion of it. He will figure out the rest as he goes along.

As Joanna began to anticipate the kids leaving, she went back to school to earn an MA in engineering. She had worked for an architectural firm as an engineer when she and Dennis started dating, putting her career aside for her family as it grew. The New Freedom period turned out to be essential for her because not only did she earn a new degree, she also grew her professional network in the process. She has recently started working full-time as an engineer. Her horizons are growing as she hoped they would. She will be on the road part of the time, but she and Dennis don't see that as a problem since they are both so excited about her professional future.

Paul Simmons's and Jack Tracy's New Horizons Story

Paul and Jack, 59 and 58, respectively, have been a couple for 23 years. Recently married, they celebrated with travel and long weekends together. Neither one wants to retire. Both are professionals who earn a good living. Their decision to get married after all these years felt surprisingly like New Freedom to both of them: the freedom to be a couple of grown-ups in a legal, respectful relationship in public and in private. What has surprised them both is the anticipation of the future that has come with this New

Freedom. In the past 23 years they have bought, remodeled, and sold 17 homes. Having had a great time doing it, somehow their New Freedom was a catalyst to decide to search for other activities they could do together. Jack and Paul are in the midst of exploring owning a boat, buying an airplane, becoming foster parents for a teenager, driving the Alcan Highway, and going to culinary school. They like the freedom, especially the powerful effect it has had on considering New Horizons for themselves.

New Simplicity

The third period I call New Simplicity. It's that period when we decide we don't want (and maybe cannot handle) so many complicating things in our lives. Large houses and their maintenance, too many relationships that don't nurture us, excessive volunteer commitments that used to be meaningful but aren't anymore, physical clutter we've held onto for too long, and dreams and intentions that no longer hold appeal or punch for us. Carl and Mona loved the big house where they had raised their family. With five bedrooms and sitting on an acre of land, it had been the home of their dreams. Somewhere along the way—probably as a result of New Freedom and New Horizons—they found they needed to make a choice. They had finite energy, time, and money. They could devote themselves to the house and acre or they could do other things that were emerging interests. Downsizing was their solution. Their kids all saw this coming before they did.

Each of these important—even essential—periods requires choices, sacrifices or letting go, and trade-offs.

Minna Stanley's New Simplicity Story

Minna and Bob Stanley, ages 72 and 74, had it all planned out. Minna finally retired three years after Bob did. She loved her work and had trouble giving it up. The couple kept their longtime Ohio home and bought a small house in a warm climate on a golf course for their winter retreats. They would rent it out the rest of the year. They had one season living in the middle of their three-phased life plan, complete with friends' visits from snowy Cleveland. Then

Minna was diagnosed with terminal cancer. Always a team of two, whether they were raising children or going to graduate school or attending to each other's health, they didn't pretend everything would be all right. Almost instantly they both yearned for greater simplicity and less physical baggage as Minna's illness progressed. Bob admitted that he dreaded going through all of their things to decide what to keep. Minna admitted she had certain things she wanted each of the kids to have, things she associated with them and that would have an extended life in their homes. By the time Minna was really sick, they had slimmed down everything to a point that Bob could handle it. Minna felt relieved that she had been able to have her hand in the upcoming New Simplicity. They both seemed very peaceful. Bob has promised to live a good and full life. He is assisted in this by the amount of simplicity they created together.

Natasha and Irving Wallace's New Simplicity Story

The Wallaces, both in their 70s, are newlyweds. Each lost a spouse about six years ago. They both owned large homes full of furniture, accrued stuff, and memories. When they became a couple, about 18 months before they married, they went back and forth about who would move into whose house, which furniture they would keep, what they would let go of, how they would go about consolidating households, and what to give to the kids. One morning they woke up, looked at each other, and said in unison, "This is dumb!" While trying to compromise to make sure the other's needs were met, it took quite a while for them to realize and admit that they would both be happier by starting fresh in a smaller home, newly furnished, that belonged to the two of them. They put their houses on the market and sold them, living temporarily in an apartment while awaiting construction of the bungalow-style house they had selected and purchased together. They had a decorator they really liked go through each of their houses and the new house plans. Together with the decorator, they selected those things they wanted to keep and had all of those things placed in storage. And then both of their houses sold within a week of each other. The new house was ready, they went through the punch-list process to make sure everything was completed, and immediately left for a three-week road trip before moving in.

While they were on the road trip, the decorator furnished the house with the new furniture and all of the things from storage they wanted to keep. The decorator also arranged for all of the remaining furnishings in their old houses, after the kids took what they wanted, to be donated and taken away when the sale closed. When Natasha and Irving arrived at their new house at the end of their trip, they left the luggage in the car, opened the front door, and tiptoed through their new simple house with simpler furniture and the treasures they had wanted to keep. They were simply home without having to deal with any of the hassles of the move or redecorating. What does this have to do with sacrifices and trade-offs? Sacrifices and trade-offs are an integral part of the learning loop decisions in Chapter 3. They are a part of the wisdom we will all need between 50 and elderly.

WE'RE ALL PIONEERS

There will always be straightaways and surprise curves on our life's roadway, sometimes a hairpin turn and sometimes a switchback and sometimes a road so straight and clear that it's obvious why no speed limit is required. Like it or not, we're all in a transition. We're all pioneers. Imagine you just stepped off a sailing ship onto a beach with a large rock. You don't know the territory. You don't know the culture. You don't know the topography. You don't know the rules. What you already know and have experienced may or may not be applicable and useful. How do you find out? You pioneer your way through transition after transition. This is increasingly what our world between 50 and elderly will require because there are so many of us, our institutions cannot be relied upon to solve things for us, and our assumptions may or may not prove to be true.

TO REPEAT: SURPRISES AND CURVES HAPPEN

There is a world of difference between being surprised by change, unable to name and see it for what it is, and being surprised by change with the knowledge, vocabulary, and insight to see what's really going on in a reasonably short period of time.

Surprises can be joyful, if shocking, sometimes. They can also bear gifts of opportunity you may not see immediately. It's not my hope to save you from surprises and curves any more than I would expect you to save me. It is my hope that throughout these chapters you increasingly have the tools to see what's really going on, work with it in manageable bites, and adapt both yourself and your plan without the crushing assumption that something must be desperately wrong and horrible. It may be difficult but you are increasingly up to it as a result of doing the work we've described in this book.

chapter 9

Learning from the Transitions
of Others

B y now I hope you are convinced that retirement—and life for that matter—isn't a one-size-fits-all concept. In the end, you have some plans to build, some decisions to make, and some actions to take.

- You have lots of money and are only concerned about planning for the qualities of your life unrelated to financial security.
- OR you have enough to consider not working at all or only working part-time to meet your life's day-to-day needs.
- OR you don't have the money saved for not working and are either unlikely to stop working or will need to significantly downscale your life.
- OR you can't imagine not working and have no desire to stop but you know for sure that, regardless, you still have planning to do because quality of life is increasingly important to you After 50.

It's called Your Life for a reason. I'm pretty optimistic about our futures; after all, people who are paying attention and have the necessary information are likely to have higher-quality lives than those who do not. Regardless of your situation and intentions, you will need to plan and adapt as part of your high-quality After 50 life.

That's what this book is all about.

After 50 we can begin to see ourselves eventually "transitioning" from our traditional and previous roles without exactly knowing where we're going or what the world is going to be like. Included in those transitions will be retirement, whatever that turns out to be for each of us. We're going to encounter moving targets and winding roads. We need plans. A key aspect of the New Normal is that we shouldn't feel like failures if part or even most of the plan doesn't work out, whether changes were forced upon us or we changed our minds. We need to know that success lies in our ability to adapt the plan and ourselves to match evolving reality, probability, and preferences.

 The best choices available to you down the road may not be the same as the ones available now. You may not have one option such as a specific job or one location or a decision answerable with a yes or no. The best choices for you may have shelf-life expiration and not be permanent. The most workable choices for you may be several selections you piece together iteratively down the sometimes curvy road.

What does this mean for us as great three-perspective planners and people who are living our lives through paying attention and adapting as necessary? What does this mean for those of us who, regardless of our future imaginations, have to find smart ways to live high-quality lives a day at a time?

A menu of choices is available. If your first and best choice is available and affordable, great. If not, don't think you have failed. Most of us, over time, will begin to cobble the best pieces together into shapes that work well for us in the short run and can be modified as we go along.

The best choices you see now may be fleeting. In fact, as we get older, there is an increasing probability that our choices will be made as part of a series rather than as independent/freestanding, permanent decisions. We won't have the satisfaction of saying to ourselves, "Phew. That's decided forever. I won't ever have to worry about that one again."

That's why you should pay attention to how other people have managed their life and retirement transition. Notice I said "pay attention," not "follow." There is no reason you or I should adopt without analysis or modification a strategy that worked for someone else. Imagine putting on a pair of shoes someone else had selected for himself/herself and buying the shoes because they fit and looked good on the other person.

So how do we go about getting access to important, usable information about other people's planning and living experiences? We ask.

Think back in the book to me saying that the world is so highly networked and fast paced now that we can't possibly know everything and everyone to whom we'll need to be connected. When I am doing career coaching with people, I encourage them to think beyond who they know personally. If you are seeking work configured as freelance or a project or a job or any of the other emerging forms of work for pay, there is a slight possibility you could go to one of your friends and ask, "Where is such a thing?" and he or she would know. There is a MUCH greater chance that you will have to go beyond your personal network to open all the necessary doors to possibilities, opportunities, and great work/person matching. This means going to people in your own network and asking them to open their own networks in a smart and informed way.

In Chapter 4, we named the asset categories—beyond financial—that you ought to have or build and refresh. I broke those assets into four categories:

1. Tangible Assets
2. Intangible Assets
3. Current Skills
4. Current Knowledge

In the Tangible Asset category, I placed this description and example:

> People to whom you are less connected *and* who possess
> skills/interests/knowledge/connections that you might need
> to tap into from time to time when your core network of
> relationships doesn't have what you need. Note: These may
> be the connection of relationships that your core network
> already has in place but you don't know about it.

Kirk and Debby's son, Pete, was in the process of choosing which
law school he should attend. Their friend Bill had a friend with
two sons who were both about 5 years out of law school. Bill
connected Pete with the two-closer to his age than Bill or his parents - law school graduates so that he could interview them about
1. what school they chose, 2. what they wish they had known in
advance, 3. what came as a pleasant surprise, and 4. what they
would choose if they had it all to do over again. Their experience
and insight to Pete proved to be so valuable that he was able to
make a clear and solid choice. All from people Pete didn't know
and to whom is now weakly connected.

Kathy, 66, was finally retired from her last full-time job: graphic
artist for an advertising business. Her heart's desire was to use
her skills to help more children with their reading abilities. On a
flight returning from a visit to her daughter and grandchildren,
she began a conversation with a younger woman seated to her
left. Kathy expressed her interest in using her graphics skills to
help with children's reading. The woman's husband, as karma
would have it, was an elementary schoolteacher. He was at home
working on a reading skills-oriented book for kids. The two ladies
made the connection. It didn't result in Kathy doing illustrations
for that book, but it did open a door for Kathy to a professional
association of children's authors and illustrators. This connection
through a connection opened doors to all kinds of opportunities
Kathy hadn't known about and wouldn't have discovered without
her awareness of weak connections and effective networking. Most
of us have key questions about retirement and life planning and
living for which publications and courses, excellent though they
may be, leave us with a few unanswered but vital questions. This is

the point at which your capacity for lifelong learning needs to kick in. This is also the point at which you need to use your Tangible Asset and ask your close connections to open the doors to their connections for you.

There are four major advantages to you building/refreshing and using this asset very well:

1. You will get additional, important perspectives.
2. You can build a bigger or more focused base from which to move and make more informed decisions.
3. You will be given gifts of information you never thought to ask about.
4. You will have confirmation that you are far from alone in your planning and in your living.

Here is how to proceed:

1. Make sure you have done a thorough job of reviewing your assets, noting where they are sufficient and insufficient, so that you have at least the rudiments of an asset improvement plan in place. See Chapter 4.
2. Make sure your life characteristics list is complete for now (and not so long that it will sink under its own weight). See Chapter 7.
3. Make sure the short-term, mid-term, and longer-term segments of your plan are well thought out and have the amount of detail and specificity appropriate to each.
4. Decide what you are unsure about and/or how you and your plan would benefit from having a conversation with someone who is ahead of you on that road.
5. Remember the qualifications for someone with whom to speak from earlier in the book: *Hint:* Pick someone you respect who is perceptive, candid, and not so close to you that his or her feedback will be diluted. If you can't think of someone, ask one of your friends for a recommendation to open the connection door for you.
6. Explain to the people you select that you are looking for insight into retirement planning. You would like to meet

with selected people for one-hour maximum at a time convenient to them. You will come prepared with questions. Although they may want the questions in advance, I encourage you not to do that because it increases the likelihood of you hearing a rehearsed speech rather than a candid telling of one's story.

7. Make the appointments. Be on time. Don't overstay the hour. If you want to go back another time, you can do that.

8. Remember that the quality of the question drives the quality of the answer.

9. Remember that great interviews are more than getting answers to your questions. They also include enough time for the other person to tell you what he/she thinks you should know that you didn't think to ask.

If all of this seems to be a lot of work, imagine how much work it is to back out of decisions and commitments because you failed to get enough of the right information early on. There are no guarantees, but all of this is very much an investment in your future. We titled the book *How Do I Get There from Here? Planning for Retirement When the Old Rules No Longer Apply* on purpose. I want you to be as successful as possible in planning, adapting, and living in times that are, to say the least, fraught with both Continuous and Discontinuous Change.

As you well know by now, it's impossible for me to give you the five questions or the six universal steps that will make everything permanent, and riskless. On the other hand, it is possible for me to give you examples of different scenarios along with possible questions.

Bob and Sally, ages 67 and 66, both a year away from leaving their jobs, have been reading magazine articles about the best places to retire. Having lived through "enough bitter Midwest winters," they are ready for a warmer climate. Bob and Sally originally planned to move to be near their son and his family, but he accepted two promotions in three years that involved substantial relocation. They quickly came to the conclusion that although it would be nice to be closer to their grandchildren, Bob and Sally didn't want to keep moving to follow them, and they also worried that their son might turn down an important promotion in the dynamic tension between his career and being loyal to them.

The list of places they liked the best based on supporting articles and information included:

Phoenix, AZ, metro area
Alexandria, VA
Tucson, AZ
Prescott, AZ
Des Moines, IA
Austin, TX
Cape Coral/Ft. Myers, FL
Colorado Springs, CO
Franklin, TN

Snow and cold weather eliminated several of these possibilities. The couple began to follow social media conversations among people who had recently moved to each of the remaining locations. At a dinner, Bob and Sally discovered through a friend of her visiting sister that the sister was great friends with someone who had moved to Austin two years ago. Through their neighbor, a local realtor, they connected with a realtor in Cape Coral who in turn connected them with two couples who had just moved there. One of Bob's customers had a branch office in Tempe, and through that connection, Bob and Sally were able to connect with three people in their own age group in the Phoenix area.

All of the people they connected with were willing to devote some time discussing their own experiences. What questions did Sally and Bob decide to ask? You've seen these questions earlier in the book. Now that you have several chapters under your belt, so to speak, are these the best questions for Sally and Bob to ask? What would you do to make these and other questions even smarter?

I realize you have seen some of these questions before.

1. When you originally thought of retirement, what did you imagine it to be?

2. What has it actually turned out to be?
3. What originally drew you to where you are now?
4. What did you wish you had known in advance?
5. What has come as a pleasant surprise?
6. What has been disappointing?
7. What are the primary ways that newcomers integrate themselves into the community over time?
8. If you had it to do over again, what would you do and why?
9. What advice would you give to anyone considering moving there?
10. What haven't we asked that we should be asking about?

The answers to these questions—from people with actual, practical experience and insight—provided the informational tipping point for Bob and Sally. Of course, before they made the final commitment to move, they visited their first-choice location. By then the people they had interviewed were their new friends who in turn introduced them to their own friends. Sally and Bob have been using the techniques of learning from others' experience ever since in a wide variety of life areas.

Chapter 10

Savoring Uncertainty

Until recently I thought about NOT writing this chapter. I didn't want to write a pep talk. I certainly didn't want to write a chapter trying to convince you to simply ignore today's chaotic world and move on into your retirement and life planning as if nothing much was going on around you that really mattered.

Then I realized what I did want to write was an unflinching look at reality: We're in a period of insecurity and change. The world isn't going to end. We're not going over a cliff. I'm not being pessimistic or hiding my head in the sand. We have retirement and life planning to do AND we're going to do our planning and our living in times of significant uncertainty for the foreseeable future.

Several years ago, I attended an ALS gala fund-raising event in northern California. I found myself seated next to John Madden, the famous football and broadcast celebrity. In the midst of telling me what it was like for him to travel so much, out of the blue he stopped and asked, "Did you ever wonder about the people who invented cottage cheese? How did they know when they were done?" At the time I laughed. Then I began to take the question more seriously. Now, years later, I still remember it. What a great and profound question! And it is such a great metaphor for life. Done may not be the ultimate measure of security and accomplishment after all. Avoiding or denying uncertainty definitely won't be.

As positive as I am about our futures, it would be unrealistic of me to pretend we aren't in a time when Continuous Change remains the dominant, primary force in our lives. Instead, we are in a time when Discontinuous Change has become the dominant, primary force. The list seems endless: climate change and its impact on our physical and economic lives; the advance of technologies that are already dramatically reshaping the world of work for pay including replacing many of what used to be lower and mid-level organizations; the shifting of power in the world as demonstrated by the jostling for global mind-share position/ dominance of disputed territories/economic power/military power/ doctrinal prominence; the understandable complaints from the millions to whom new forms of wealth/security/health and hopeful futures have failed to trickle down; "terrorism" coming from foreigners and from our own citizens as a force in the world and in our nation that doesn't appear to be going away any time soon; our apparent dissatisfaction with and suspicion of all three branches of government (executive, legislative, judicial); the increasing globalization of professional and personal communities and communication through the Internet and other technologies that in many ways are rendering historic cultural and geographic boundaries irrelevant; great advances in genetics that could give us longer lives without the capacity to pay for them or the emerging interests and abilities that would make them very high quality; the recent acceleration in the decline of public civility as demonstrated by political races at all levels; the significant decline in religion/church-based life in favor of values-driven lives rooted in "spirituality"; and the hollowing out of the middle class and—just as important—the evaporation of middle-class work for pay that created both the dream and the ability to pursue it in a grounded, stable fashion. It's a prodigious list and it isn't even a complete one.

In the middle of all of this we're supposed to be doing intelligent retirement and life planning? YES! And in the middle of this—not to mention the simple attributes of our own aging, changes in interests and relationships, and the decreasing time horizon within which we can reasonably plan in detail and permanence—we can reasonably expect our lives and the lives of those we love not to be discontinuously affected somehow? *No!*

Regardless of financial capacity, it isn't reasonable to assume we and those we care about are somehow inviolably insulated and protected from discontinuous forces in our lives.

It also isn't reasonable to assume we are doomed and, therefore, smart planning, living, and adapting is pointless because it's all too out of control and going to end badly anyway.

As I said, I'm especially interested in all of us finding ways to do smart, reasonable planning and adapt ourselves and our plans as we go along.

Going back to savoring uncertainty, let's take a closer look.

Savoring means to appreciate fully, to enjoy or relish, especially in taste or smell. Given the fact it's a metaphor, when, in the normal course of your life, you think of or encounter uncertainty, what does it taste and smell like?

Reader Exercise

Answer the following questions:

1. What was one important life situation that you savored?
2. How did you know savoring was a possibility in that situation?
3. What did it smell and taste like and what was your visceral experience of it?
4. How did this savoring inform other possibilities for savoring in the future?
5. How good are you now at being aware of the possibility of savoring in the moment and stopping to do it?
6. How good at it will you need to be as you move into your retirement and future?

Uncertainty involves situations for which we have only imperfect and/or unknown information. It applies to predictions of future events, environments, or events that are only partly observable, and experiences about which you're ignorant. (You're not stupid but you lack the necessary information or education.)

The life of Judith Sedgeman, EdD, for the past three decades has been centered in her dedication to awakening creativity, resiliency, and well-being in people through their understanding of the Principles of Mind, Thought, and Consciousness, which are the foundations of our experience of innate health. She is a teacher, mentor, and consultant in that work. (More about Judy can be found at http://www.three-principles.com.)

When I interviewed Judy Sedgeman, we both wanted to include her favorite subject: innate health. Here is a segment of our conversation:

George: Suppose an assortment of people came into your living room and said, "We're 50 and have completed many if not most of the things we set out to do. Where do we go from here?" How would you advise them?

Judy: Well, the first thing I would say is, don't be afraid. I would teach them not to be afraid, not to follow fearful thoughts, and not to look in the mirror. I have clients who say, well, I'm too old to try this or that. You're only too old if you think you're too old. If you're infirm, you have limitations. But if you're not infirm, try it, you know?

So the first thing I would do is share what I understand about our thinking. How we take thinking on, and how seriously we take it, and how easily we get led astray by the thoughts we've borrowed from other people. Like, "You shouldn't do that." Like people over 50 shouldn't wear blue jeans. There are a lot of ideas that especially women have— but a lot of men have ideas, too—about what's appropriate, what's not, what they should be doing at this point in their lives, and what they shouldn't be doing. What would people think? What if I don't do well and then I have my first so-called failure?

Failure is a thought. You could call it a learning experience and move on. But calling it failure kind of makes it icky. So I would work there first. I'd help you to free your mind from all these habitual, self-defeating, self-limiting thoughts that we've accumulated over a lifetime, that are or are just thoughts. They don't have any power except the power that we give them.

And then I would start talking to people about, what's something that you always wished that you had done, but you never had time for? You didn't get around to it? And you'd be surprised. I've actually done this with people, and you'd be surprised what they come up with. I was talking the other day to somebody who had to retire from nursing because she really couldn't spend that much time on her feet anymore. She had some kind of medical issue, but she's very vibrant and a really wonderful person. And I said, what's something that you always kind of had in the back of your mind that you just never had time for, or never gotten to do?

And she said, "You know, ever since I was little, because I love books so much, I thought I'd like to write stories for children." But she had never really brought that thought to the foreground because she got busy and got into her life. And I said, well, what kind of stories would you want to write? And she said, "Well, I don't know. When I was little, I just thought I could do this."

Reader Exercise

Answer the following questions.

1. What was one important life situation in which uncertainty appeared?
2. How did you know you were uncertain?
3. What did it smell and taste like and what was your visceral experience of it?
4. How did you see and work with it?
5. As you do your retirement and life planning, what is uncertain that you must see and work with right now?
6. How good will you need to be at seeing and working with uncertainty as you move into your retirement and life futures?

Let's take a look at four scenarios in which you can look for opportunities to savor as well as possible uncertainties.

Bill and Doris Green, ages 63 and 64, both worked for the same company straight out of college. When the kids came along, Doris left to be a stay-at-home mom. Bill changed employers twice, both times for significant promotions in manufacturing management. Pensions and defined benefit plans had, of course, gone away. In their place, the Greens made it a priority to put money into 401(K)s and employer matching plans as well as building a significant equity in their home over time. When he was 54, with two kids in college, Bill's company was sold, his job was declared "redundant," and he was laid off. Despite his best efforts, Bill was unable to land another comparable job. They lived on their savings. Eventually Doris went to work in retail and Bill went back to school for retraining in technologies. It was a tough time. Their kids are now out of college. Both Doris and Bill are employed. Tearfully, they sold their house at the top of the market and now rent an apartment, which to their great surprise, has proved to be a happy change. They have rebuilt some of their savings but certainly not enough for them to stop working. As they look toward "retirement," it looks increasingly like eventual part-time work for both of them combined with local interests and activities. Their biggest retirement worry is outliving their money. Retirement isn't a new and discrete phase of life in their future. It's an integrated and logical extension of the decisions they are making and the life they are living now.

Reader Exercise

Answer the following questions:

1. What do Doris and Bill have to savor?
2. What do Doris and Bill have to be uncertain about?
3. If they came to you for words of wisdom or advice, what would you say to them?

Sixty-six-year-old Barbara Kushner thought she and her husband had it all together financially and personally. They had just retired to Arizona from Ohio. She was looking forward to music, golf, and a life of volunteering and good works. Then Tom, her husband, suddenly passed away. Barbara had never paid attention to the financial side of their lives. Tom took care of all of that. When he died, she was suddenly propelled into a relationship with a financial advisor she didn't know, a set of unfamiliar financial concepts and languages, and a combination of decisions she wasn't prepared to make yet couldn't delay. It turned out that Tom had made two unwise investments that, in fact, had cost them a large portion of their net worth. She certainly isn't going to lose the house, and she won't be destitute. However, she will have to downscale her lifestyle in order to live within her means. For Barbara, retirement will involve learning a whole body of financial knowledge she should have had earlier, working part-time, and gathering her friends and family around her to help her make the transitions necessary.

Reader Exercise

Answer the following questions:

1. What does Barbara have to savor?
2. What does Barbara have to be uncertain about?
3. If she came to you for words of wisdom or advice, what would you say to her?

....

Carol Folsom and Rick Smedley, both 68, met in law school years ago. Married early, they both pursued high-powered, well-paid professional careers. When their daughter came along, they readily adapted to sharing responsibility for her along with a full-time nanny. Their daughter grown and gone, they are both at the top of their careers and beginning to execute on their retirement plan. Carol and Rick had worked intensely hard for years, largely buffered by their professions from the business roller coaster beyond their doors. They are going to keep their condo in Chicago but have also purchased a condo in Florida. They plan winters in Florida and summers at home. Money is not an issue. Having been active and financially able philanthropists for years, they are moving a portion of their money to a community foundation in Florida, which will automatically make them members of an elite community of donors and nonprofit board members. Rick is buying a boat. Carol is joining a tennis club. They are both planning on taking lifelong learning classes. Retirement for Rick and Carol looks like the ability to step into communities and interests that will provide them with new stimulation and friendships. Now if they could just get Rick's arrhythmia to go away . . .

Reader Exercise

Answer the following questions:

1. What do Carol and Rick have to savor?
2. What do Carol and Rick have to be uncertain about?
3. If they came to you for words of wisdom or advice, what would you say to them?

Ted Dawson, 72, failed retirement, not once but twice! Divorced and unsettled at age 55, he jumped on the opportunity to retire, thinking it would be a fresh and wonderful relaunch for him. With his kids' support he visited 15 of the cities featured in *99 Best Places to Retire*, did the necessary research through friends of friends already in these places, chose the best one for him, bought a house, and moved. This all happened quickly after he announced he was retiring from dentistry. During the first year in his new home and city, Ted volunteered widely. He worked at developing nonprofit board expertise. He threw small dinner parties for other retirees in his neighborhood. Eventually he realized that part-time volunteering wasn't enough in his case and that he needed to find a full-time job. For four years he became the executive director of a local nonprofit. When he had taken the organization as far as he could take it, he retired again. Six months later, he felt himself to be floundering again, clearly wanting something he could own.

On top of that he, somewhat surprisingly, found himself increasingly ambivalent about being part of a couple again, something that until recently he had quietly longed for. The ownership solution turned out to come with an opportunity to buy into a local dental practice and work three days a week, effectively job sharing with another dentist who wanted ownership and part-time practice, too. For Ted, retirement looks like a combination of ownership, part-time practice, volunteering, and uncommitted time.

Reader Exercise

Answer the following questions:

1. What does Ted have to savor?
2. What does Ted have to be uncertain about?
3. If he came to you for words of wisdom or advice, what would you say to him?

When you first saw this chapter's title, "Savoring Uncertainty," what did you think? It's my guess that many of you rolled your eyes and thought, "Oh, right, sure!"

I hope that you realize I don't intend to:

1. Pretend uncertainty is a significant source of pleasure to be reveled in.
2. Convince you that should you trick yourself into pretending uncertainty is anything other than what it is.
3. Harangue you about facing up because I am afraid you will rapidly come down with some voluntary combination of denial and dementia around uncertainty.

Instead, I am encouraging you to take a clear look at uncertainty to see what it really is and isn't about and what you can reasonably do about it and with it. Of course, by definition, there are parts of uncertainty you can't see. You won't be able to reasonably do anything about those parts except to keep them in perspective, ask for support and assistance when you need it (hiding out with our own uncertainty as a dark secret for extended periods of time is unlikely to be good for us), and, especially, keep looking at your own success stories and methods in adapting to both Continuous and Discontinuous Change.

chapter 11

How Will I Know When I'm Done?

THE DONE TEST

There is a very simple and easy test for this. If you are dead, you're done. If you are still alive and managing your affairs and life (even with a bit of assistance), you aren't done. Just check your pulse, respiration, and who is primarily responsible for your life. That will tell you whether you're done.

Of course, this will require letting go of the illusion that there is such a place as a permanent and irrefutable life destination at which to arrive.

LEARNING NEEDS TO BE LIFELONG

I also think the decisions and efforts we make in the period between age 50 and elderly dramatically affect the quality of our lives not only during that period but during the elderly period also. A great 60-year-old existence doesn't begin at age 58. A great life for a 90-year-old doesn't begin at age 88. They are called Lifelong

Learning and Human Development for a reason. Learning absolutely must be a lifelong activity, given everything going on around us and the inevitability of it affecting ourselves or our loved ones.

Argentine Saunders Craig, PhD, now 80, was and is a significant mentor for me. She was the chairwoman of my doctoral dissertation committee when I was getting my PhD. She famously stared down the rest of the committee at the very end, when some wanted late changes in design, by using a deeply understood Peace Corps village and drinking water metaphor. She quietly looked toward them and asked, "Whose well is this, anyway?" As a lifelong learner she has endless stories to tell. Should you see her, ask her how she helped Nelson Mandela to be elected the first time. And then there was the time she and I went to lunch in San Francisco. As we were being led to our table, she and Bishop Desmond Tutu greeted each other warmly. When I interviewed her for this book, I was yet again reminded of the learning power of stories.

Nominally retired, Dr. Craig continues to demonstrate the power of lifelong learning.

George: So you're retired. Uh-huh!

Argentine: You know; I say that I'm retired but I ... I'm retired from the university. As you know, I retired in 2000, the year my granddaughter was born. However, I continued to consult in the field of my expertise, Applied Behavioral Science and Human Development, because of contacts and contracts. I just wasn't officially connected with the university anymore. I did participate as an instructor in a course— Diversity in International Consulting—and we took the group to consult with the government in Bermuda. And then there was another international consulting course that involved a university, connections with the Trinidad and Tobago governments, and taking students to Amsterdam for an international consulting experience. My academic title all this time was Professorial Lecturer. Who said retirement means the end of learning? I think I learned almost as much as the students because every situation and context is different. You have to be on your toes the whole time. I learned and they learned. Now, this is after I retired, you know, from the university. I didn't stop working in my area of expertise. But it was at a pace and in places that worked for me. And lifelong learning is a part of it for all of us. Yes!

THE GOAL AND ROLE TRAP

I touched on this topic earlier, but want to emphasize it here.

We've grown up in a diverse (even if we weren't exposed to it) and significantly goal-oriented nation that often employs opposites such as Yes or No, Democrat or Republican, Black or White, Win or Lose, and short-term problem solving rather than employing deeper, more difficult, and more time-consuming thinking that requires perspectives, trying short-term alternatives, and changing our minds.

 Many of us, given the culture we've grown up in, are deeply suspicious of NOT having goals, even if that goal is a goal-free life of leisure. There doesn't seem to be much happy medium ground. Either we've got goals galore or we don't want anything to do with them for now.

Upon traditional retirement (think pension, leisure, far fewer responsibilities) it's fairly easy to set goals and roles aside because it's a highly ritualized transition in which we are giving things up anyway, so why not goals and roles? If our lives aren't about goals and roles, what on earth is left?

I'm not suggesting you throw out all your goals and roles. I am suggesting, however, that as we age we will need to move to another core by which to evaluate and validate ourselves and our lives. And now, when we're considering which faces of retirement we want to create for ourselves in the short-term, mid-term, and long-term ranges, is a great time to develop our facility for knowing and validating ourselves outside of goals and roles.

Much later in our lives, let's be honest, the number of and size of achievable goals we can set for ourselves will be more limited. Also, the number of roles we can fill (and are asked to fill) will also diminish. It was a really big deal when a friend's mother, age 79, finally gave up on having Christmas Eve at her house every year complete with sit-down dinner for 14. This had been both a goal and a role for her since her kids were adolescents. It gave her pleasure, identity, a sense of achievement, and an anchor for her identity as mother, grandmother, and aunt. It also had come to give her anxiety, exhaustion, and a kind of peevishness her kids had never seen before.

What are the tools and processes for adding a better long-term possibility to our way of knowing ourselves and judging our value?

THE BENEFITS OF LIFE CHARACTERISTICS

My answer to that question lies in the list of characteristics you chose as representative of your future life. You chose them. You can update and improve them as you go along. They are less likely than goals and roles to depend upon others for fruition. They are essential indicators of how on track your life and your plan are. They are also key indicators that you and/or your plan need adapting or updating.

Comparing your Life Characteristics List to your actions, decisions, relationship interactions, intentions, and patterns will give you immediate feedback. You don't need anyone else to do this, although you may want to use a friend as a sounding board (much as I've suggested several times in this book) or you may prefer to speak with a professional advisor.

Some people orient themselves and their lives based on a values framework, a value-based life. I applaud this, as well as remembering our values in all intentions and transactions. From my standpoint, values answer the question HOW as in, "How am I treating others?" I totally support that framework as a part of what we need BUT I don't think it takes us all the way to where we need to go. Values, in my experience, always require that you interact with others. For example, you show kindness to others, loyalties to your families and nation, and honesty in your business dealings with others. It's hard to practice them all by ourselves when their intended purpose is to inform our interaction with others. I am not dismissing values here, nor am I suggesting they not be a valuable subtext for life characteristics.

What I am saying, however, is that the characteristics you have chosen will be the gold standard against which you measure your progress and success. From my standpoint, the characteristics serve as your life's North Star. They are the WHO and WHAT, as in "Who am I becoming?" and "What is my life like/what will it be like?" No one else owns them. You don't need anyone else to measure them. They are highly shareable with your family and friends, yet they remain irretrievably yours. It's called your life for a reason. Only you can decide what you want it to be like or characterized by. And only you can change your life characteristics as appropriate. In the meantime, like a list hung on the refrigerator, you can use the list in your head in anticipating upcoming opportunities and making congruent/beneficial choices.

A CHANCE TO PRACTICE

Willa Bernhard is a friend of mine. She is in a women's organization with my wife, Linda, and that is how we met. How we really got to know each other, however, was when we were doing some volunteer work together and agreed we didn't like the approved process. She's a New Yorker transplanted to Sarasota, FL. At 88, she still claims she has had a lot of happy accidents that have guided her life. After having kids, she got a masters in guidance and counseling, taught at Sarah Lawrence, then earned a PhD and became a psychologist-therapist, eventually dealing in sexual disorders, which all began with "meeting a woman doctor who had just written a big book on sex therapy" who ended up taking her into her practice at New York Hospital. And that ended up with Willa doing some teaching at Cornell Medical School. I mean this woman is amazing. What does this all have to do with a Chance to Practice? Willa and her husband, Bob, age 90, moved from a beautiful beachfront condo to a "retirement community or whatever you want to call it." When she retired early in her 70s, Willa wanted to know, "What do women do when they retire?" So she made a list of questions, networked through her friends (everyone knew a "fantastic woman" for her to interview), and ended up doing 100 amazing interviews that became an article published in journals and that turned into—again by accident—being picked up by a woman who was running "Women on the Web."

When I interviewed Willa, we discussed the important themes of her retirement investigation and what she learned from making the move from the condo to where she and Bob are now.

George: What were the dominant themes you discovered?

Willa: Every one of the women felt that they were feeling far better about themselves than they had when they were younger.

George: It's all right, I was really looking for what the themes were that impressed you, or struck you the most. Specifically, that would have informed your own decisions. You went back and forth a lot between Florida and New York for a long time, almost as if commuting between segments of your life.

Willa: What would have informed my decisions . . . It was certainly that life does get better for women. And that was certainly true for me; from my mid-40s on, my life really opened up. So I used that when I was treating women for therapy. Women would come in and say, "I'm turning 60!" and I would say, "It's the beginning of the best time of your life." And I really believe that.

George: So in all this coming and going and the transitions . . . I'm interested in how you re-crafted your sense of yourself.

Willa: Everything in my life . . . well, it was planned that I would go back and get a degree. But other than that, everything in my life really was that a door . . . sort of opened for me, and I went through it. So I did not have the kind of plan where you decide early on you're going to be a lawyer and you follow that kind of path.

George: So here you are at 88. I get how you made the transition to your condo here. How about making the transition into this "retirement community or whatever you call it" a year and a half ago?

Willa: That was a big surprise. Bob and I really were happy with our life. We had a beautiful apartment and we liked it, but we knew that at some point in your life you should probably transition. And everybody said you should do it before you have problems. And we very reluctantly did it. We had a lot of "Will we?" "Should we?" "No, we don't want to." Bob would take one position and I would take another. And then finally we decided that, I mean, what am I now, 88? I was beginning to be 87. Bob is two years older than I am. And so we made the jump. I knew that it was really important, if you're going to a retirement facility, to be in the middle of things, because to be way out someplace is a disadvantage. It wouldn't be so much of a disadvantage right now, because we drive. But at that point you don't drive anymore; you're cut off from this community. So here we are about two blocks from everything. And not only do they take you to things if you need them to, Bob has been to three meetings today and I've been to one meeting today, it's very accessible and I think that's really, really important.

Paula and Joe, both age 84, had a lovely home overlooking the Pacific Ocean in Southern California. They were perfectly content. They both still drove and they had two cars, so coordinating schedules and getting in and out of their steep, hillside community was no problem. Joe was retired but Paula still worked part-time on her long-standing TV show on which she interviewed politicians, artists, authors, and officials about their work and how it was changing. Happy as they were in their home and life, the couple had begun to run hot and cold in their conversations about letting nature take its course and forcing them—with the assistance of their grown kids who would probably shoulder much of the burden—to move when they had no choice OR being proactive and making the majority of their own decisions now, even though it meant all the work of finding a new location, way of living, figuring out what to keep from the house, allowing for transportation that didn't have to involve driving, and making the best of it as a good thing to do at their age and stage.

Pretend for a moment that you are a professional advisor to Paula and Joe. When will they be done? How would you help them choose characteristics for their future based on making good choices and establishing priorities instead of the more common route of making the move and then naming characteristics that would now be true?

Kim is 88. Twenty years ago, when her husband died and she was face-to-face with her future, she went back to school to take writing classes. It was her plan to develop marketable skills she could use wherever she was for years and years to come. Kim is now working on her 11th book. She is especially fond of the spy and the private detective genres and still has the same agent she sought out when she was much younger. Six months ago, she took a major fall. Her biggest fear is of falling again.

Pretend for a moment that you are a professional advisor to Kim. When will she be done? How would you advise her on a smart combination of characteristics, goals, and roles?

Sixty-eight-year-old Bill retired eight years ago following an injury to one of his legs. An extroverted salesman, he has never learned to be alone with much grace. His mornings are spent at the local coffeehouse with his buddies discussing sports, restaurants, and health. They all bring their dogs. Then Bill goes home to take a nap until lunch. His afternoons are spent puttering around the house until cocktail time and dinner at home or at a restaurant with friends. Each day is similar to others. He is embarrassed by his limitations and recognizes that he needs a challenge. Pretend for a moment that you are a professional advisor to Bill. When will he be done? How would you advise him on a smart combination of characteristics, goals, and roles?

Although they are only in their early 70s, Fred and Callie, who retired seven years ago, have in many ways retired from life and are coasting to the end. For some people, "done" begins with retirement. For them, the difficult work of life is completed, it's time for Golden Years, coasting, and a well-earned extended vacation. What do you think? They are completely unaware that anyone else would ever see them as coasting. They think their lives have taken their natural course, and perhaps they have. When will Fred and Callie be really done?

Suzanne is 90 years old. Her husband died several years ago. At some point she gave up and let her daughter do her thinking and planning for her. Her daughter has now placed her in an extended-care facility because of her limited mobility. She cannot navigate going to the bathroom by herself. Physically cared for but dramatically understimulated intellectually, Suzanne spends her time watching television and receding into her memories. She is in one of those facilities that are apparently the last stop, a kind of warehouse euphemistically called "God's Waiting Room." When visitors come to see her, it takes a few minutes for the "real Suzanne"—known for her spunkiness and her humor—to come forward and join the guests. What do you think? When will Suzanne be done? Suppose Suzanne came to you for counsel and advice. Where would you start?

Barbara is 66. She and her husband recently retired at the same time with grand plans for having at least 20 years of play time together after all those years of hard work juggling careers and several children. Six months after their retirement, her husband was diagnosed with lung and brain cancer. Within a year, he was dead. Fortunately, several of Barbara's kids and grandkids live nearby. She has crafted a temporary life that's about them, knowing full well she's going to have to develop a bigger life on her own.

Pretend for a moment that you are a professional advisor to Barbara. How would you advise her on a smart combination of characteristics, goals, and roles? When will she be done?

VISITING DONE ONE MORE TIME

As a society we are in wide disagreement about when Done happens. Which is the definition of Done you are consciously or unconsciously choosing for yourself? How do you expect these decisions to affect your long-term future?

On this journey between 50 and elderly, I know I'm not alone because you're there reading. You aren't alone because I'm here researching and writing and speaking. This is a pioneering era full of transitions. Together we can figure it out individually and collectively. I sincerely hope the content of this book will make a big difference for you.

And thanks for reading to the end.

None of us will be done until we're done.

SAMPLE PLACE-TO-START
QUESTIONNAIRE

Two requests from the author:

1. If you skimmed the book to this point, go back and read it thoroughly. Do the exercises. If you don't, it will be like starting out on a car trip without knowing which pedals and levers achieve what. When you have done that, come back and use this Sample Place-to-Start Questionnaire and the Planning and Action Template that follows. It's called Your Life for a reason. You and your life deserve the best effort possible.
2. Each and every time you aren't quite sure if you are doing it "right," go back and reread the related portion of the book to refresh your memory and knowledge. There is no single "right" way to do it, but this book gives you great tools and information that will make it much easier over time.

As you know by now, I am really bullish about our retirements and our lives. Even though it seems more unknown than we are accustomed to or wish it to be, I don't think the future is scary or especially dangerous. I do, however, think it can't and won't simply be a continuing extension of our pasts. We are much more likely to experience our future as a series of overlapping, pliable periods or circumstances than we are to experience our future as a solid, unwavering roadway from here to there with little deviation or surprise. This means being organized and paying attention is necessary. And the person most responsible for doing this is you.

It would be much simpler if we could just memorize the five necessary steps of something and then execute without having to think about it too much, wouldn't it? There are places in our lives where it works to do this—for instance, lifting a fork or spoon to your mouth without spilling, walking into a room and turning a light switch to on, tying your shoes, opening the refrigerator door, looking to see if you have text or phone messages, drinking a glass of iced tea, or putting on your shirt or blouse. What do all of these have in common?

1. They are frequent/repetitive. How many times in your life have you pushed the button on the TV remote to turn it on or off? How many times have you driven to the store or to work using the same route, realizing when you arrive that you don't remember seeing much, if anything, along the way?
2. You have done them so often that you don't have to think about them. And you can get consistently away with doing them successfully well without much, if any, concentration or extra effort.
3. The environment in which they happen is highly stable. Even if you bought a new refrigerator, and instead of one door opening to the side you had two doors opening from the middle, repetition would soon overcome your previous habit, and the onetime change of refrigerator doors would rapidly recede into the cluster of things to which you don't have to give a thought. The refrigerator would be in the same place and so would the kitchen.

The future you create for yourself—in retirement and in your life overall—will be crafted in a time that is already full of Continuous and Discontinuous Change. You will see change in all the dimensions of your environment, from political to health to financial to educational to professional to networks of relationships. You will also see change in yourself as you grow and change across your entire life span. Your needs and priorities will shift, sometimes subtly and sometimes dramatically, with and without your permission. You will need to pay close and regular attention to where you are AND build a plan in the three phases we discussed at length earlier in the book.

As I have said so many times in this book, the quality of the question drives the quality of the answer.

It's easy—and a trap—in my judgment to begin this process with the details of your life. (You don't like your boss. You need to go back to school but have been putting it off. Your son just dented the car. The roof leaks. You are about to have your 50th birthday and have a sense of pressure you haven't experienced until now.) It's better to begin with the bigger picture first. I mean, the bigger picture of what really is right now, not your imagination of what you would like it to be.

Let's begin with clusters of related, big-picture questions:

- *Cluster 1:* What consistently gives you the most joy? How permanent is it? How and when is it likely to decrease or go away, given the progression of your life? How prepared are you to alter or replace it? Who else is involved in making decisions around this?

- *Cluster 2:* What in your life can you control with assurance? What can you only influence? How wise are you at regularly discerning between the two? What is an example of when you were wise? What is an example of when you were not?

- *Cluster 3:* What consistently gives you the most aggravation? How permanent is it? How and when is it likely to decrease or go away, given the progression of your life? How prepared are you to take action to alter or replace it? Who else is involved in making decisions around this?

- *Cluster 4:* Whose life or lives are so intertwined with yours that any major decision you make about your own life will automatically affect theirs? How well do you communicate with him/her/them about important topics and how well does he/she/they communicate with you about important topics?

- *Cluster 5:* If I walked up to you and asked you who you are, how would you answer the question? How satisfied are you with the answer? How much of your identity answer is made up of information outside of you, dependent on external situations and factors? How much of your identity answer is made up of information inside of you, dependent upon you only?

- *Cluster 6:* Across the years until now, how clear and organized a plan have you had for your life? In what ways has your life gone according to plan? In what ways has your life not gone according to plan? How facile have you been at adapting to voluntary and involuntary changes and deviations from the plan?

- *Cluster 7:* What worries you the most? How much energy does worrying about it siphon off from what you need each day? What would be the outcome if it happened? How would it affect your retirement and life plan? What might adapting have to look like for you and for your plan?
- *Cluster 8:* Do you yearn for something in large or small ways? What is it? How long has this yearning been with you? What would be the cost of obtaining or accomplishing it? What would be the impact on your current life?

As hardball as these questions appear to be, asking them all and answering them to the best of your current ability is really an important data and reality platform for your retirement and life planning work.

Now go back to Chapter 4: "Getting Real: Imagine Your Future and Start Planning."

When you were reading Chapter 4, did you take the time to thoughtfully do the assessment of assets that is described in detail? If you did, great! You can now, having read the remainder of the book, do a review of your assessment to see if anything has changed or if you would change/update any pieces of it as a result of what you learned in the chapters that followed.

When you were reading Chapter 4, did you decide to read the rest of the book thoroughly before going back to thoughtfully complete the Sample Asset List (Figure 4-1)? If you did, great! Now it's time to go back to Chapter 4 and complete the assessment carefully.

Either way, your thoughtful answers to the clusters of questions above, plus the completed asset assessment, ALMOST qualify you to move on to Planning and Action.

The one remaining step is to do a thorough review of your current financial status AND your anticipated financial needs in view of and informed by your completed cluster question answers and your asset assessment. As I said earlier in the book, I'm not a financial professional, but I do believe in using them. It's my strong recommendation that you do this with a credentialed financial advisor. You can use the selection criteria I explained in Chapter 4. You need not sign up to buy securities or programs with this person, the equivalent of an ongoing financial relationship at this time. You could simply buy a small number of hours—as you would with an attorney or an architect in the planning/exploration phase of a process or project—as a way to begin to have the important conversations you might not have had until now. If you are a couple, both of you should fully participate in all conversations and decision making. This might cost some money up front BUT is likely to be far less expensive than finding out considerably down the road that you failed to seize an opportunity or option because you didn't know it was available to you. If tax planning is likely to be an important part of your financial planning, you should consider buying some time from a tax expert also.

SAMPLE PLANNING AND
ACTION TEMPLATE

This is the template I recommend (see Figure A-1).

It serves two major functions:

1. It gives you a structure/framework for imagination, thinking, and action.
2. It gives you a new way to plan your future that will form, when used regularly, a method of "seeing" your future and the plan for it.

Here are some recommendations to help you take maximum advantage of the Planning and Action Template:

1. Don't do it alone. You can, of course, begin on your own, but regular reality checks—to solicit opinions and simply hear yourself talk your way through it—will be essential. Use the guidelines I cited earlier in the book to help you select someone to be your sounding board and/ or use a nonfinancial professional advisor.
2. Work the template from left to right. Let your imagination do its best to help you with your desired life characteristics.
3. Understand from the beginning that you are working in three time phases. The more distant you are from today in your planning, the less concrete the information is likely to be.
4. Be prepared to update your plan regularly. As new

information comes in that helps you create a clearer course and make better decisions, use it well.

5. Remember that success is likely to be measured in how well you adapt the plan to changing circumstances and how well you, yourself, adapt.

Figure A-1. Planning and action template.

	Desired Life Characteristics	Important Goals and Unrealized Ambitions	Thorough Review of All Four Categories of Current Assets Plus Financials	Asset Improvement Needs
Short-Term Plan 1-18 Months				
Mid-Term Plan 18-48 Months				
Long-Term Intentions 48-96 Months				

Figure A-1 (cont.)

	Asset Improvement Action Plan	What to Keep and What to Let Go Of	Establishment/ Review of Priorities	Action Plan with Action Steps and Due Dates	Plan and New, Relevant Information; Review/Plan and Planner Adaptability and Update as Necessary
Short-Term Plan 1-18 Months					
Mid-Term Plan 18-48 Months					
Long-Term Intentions 48-96 Months					

IN CLOSING

My very best wishes to you for successful planning and action. May your life be truly characterized by what you have selected.

You can find additional, insightful information at www.georgeschofield.com.

If you would like to write to me about your own story, what you've learned that was especially important to you, and/or how the process could be made even better, please feel free to contact me at george@georgeschofield.com.

NOTES

1. https://www.census.gov/prod/2010pubs/p25-1138.pdf;
   http://finovate.com/new-report-aarp-explores-longevity-economy;
   http://blog.aarp.org/2014/05/14top-10-demographics-interests-facts-
   about-americans-age-50/.
2. https://www.census.gov/prod/2014pubs/p25-1141.pdf;
   http://opi.mt.gov/pub/rti/EssentialComponents/Leadership/Present/
   Understanding%20Generational%20Differences.pdf.
3. http://www.prb.org/Publications/Media-Guides/2016/aging-
   unitedstates-fact-sheet.aspx;
   https://www.cbpp.org/research/federal-budget/program-spending-
   historically-low-outside-social-security-and-medicare.
4. http://www.aarp.org/content/dam/aarp/research/surveys/
   statistics/general/2014/Getting-to-Know-Americans-Age-50-Plus-
   Demographics-AARP-res-gen.pdf; http://blog.aarp.org/2014/05/14/
   top-10-demographics-interests-facts-about-americans-age-50/.
5. https://www.census.gov/prod/2014pubs/p25-1140.pdf; http://www.prb.
   org/Publications/Media-Guides/2016/aging-unitedstates-fact-sheet.aspx;
   http://www.pewresearch.org/fact-tank/2016/03/31/10-demographic-
   trends-that-are-shaping-the-u-s-and-the-world.
6. http://www.nirsonline.org/index.
   php?option=content&task=view&id=768; http://www.pewresearch.
   org/fact-tank/2016/06/20/more-older-americans-are-working-and-
   working-more-than-they-used-to/; http://www.businessinsider.com/
   how-much-average-family-saved-for-retirement-2016-3.
7. https://www.shrm.org/resourcesandtools/hr-topics/benefits/pages/
   retirement-postponed.aspx; https://www.shrm.org/resourcesandtools/
   hr-topics/benfits/pages/working-in-retirement.aspx; http://
   familiesandwork.org/downloads/2014NationalStudyOfEmployers.pdf.
8. https://www.ml.com/publish/content/application/pdf/GWMOL/
   MLWM/Work-in-Retirement/2014.pdf.

9. https://am.jpmorgan.com/blobcontent/1416024089049/83456/RI/Longevity/2015/final/inst.pdf.

10. https://www.ebri.org/; http://www.reuters.com/article/us-column-miller-retirement-idUSKCNOW02PE; https://www.ebri.org/pdf/briefspdf/EBRI/IB/397/Mar14.RCS.pdf.

11. http://www.gao.gov/assets/680/676942.pdf; http://www.gao.gov/products/GAO-16-242.

12. https://www.census.gov/prod/2014pubs/p25-1141.pdf.

INDEX